Blessed Are the Cynical

Blessed Are the Cynical

How Original Sin Can Make America a Better Place

Mark Ellingsen

Brazos Press
A Division of Baker Book House Co
Grand Rapids, Michigan 49516

Published by Brazos Press
A division of Baker Book House Company
P.O. Box 6287, Grand Rapids, MI 49516–6287
http://www.brazospress.com

Printed in the United States of America

Library of Congress Cataloging-in-Publication Data
Ellingsen, Mark, 1949–
    Blessed are the Cynical: How Original Sin Can Make America a Better Place /
Mark Ellingsen.
        p.   cm.
    Includes bibliographical references and index.
    ISBN 1-58743-042-8
    1. Christianity and Culture—United States. 2. Narcissism—Social Aspects—
United States. 3. Common Sense—Social Aspects—United States. 4. Augustine,
Saint, Bishop of Hippo. 5. Sin, Original—History of Doctrines—Early Church,
ca. 30–600. Common Sense—Religious aspects—Christianity—History of doc
trines—Early church, ca. 30–600. I. Title.

BR526 .E55 2003
233′.14′0973—dc21
                                                                        2002014968

To Betsey
my main partner in scholarship
my true partner in life

Contents

Acknowledgments   9
Introduction: American Society in the New Century:
    Whatever Happened to Original Sin?   13

1. The Augustinian Understanding of Reality   33
2. Augustinian Realism and the American Constitutional
    System   51
3. Politics with Glitz, but without Much Constitutional
    Common Sense   69
4. A Business-Driven Society: Whatever Happened to a Real
    Quality of Life?   99
5. Religion and the Real World: An Entertaining Religious
    Life without Sin and Guilt   119
6. Sex, Marriage, and Family without
    Common Sense   141
7. Augustinian Common Sense in
    the American Classroom   159

Conclusion: Augustinian Common Sense: The High
    Costs of Its Neglect   181

Notes   189
Index   206

Acknowledgments

Like any author, I like to think that the ideas in this book are original. But, of course, I did not write this book alone. I was leaning on the poll results and the insights of the social analysts regularly cited. And when it comes to this page, I am downright repetitious, thanking most of the same people I thank regularly in all my books. That's because certain people and institutions have shaped my life so profoundly.

This time I mention a few new names. I start with my new friend Rodney Clapp, the editorial director of Brazos Press. He has enthusiastically and very professionally encouraged and refined my work. In a way, he is not that new a friend, for it seems that we have known of each other for a number of years through the exchange of thoughts that transpired when we read each other's work.

A few other names I mention now are new, though I have gratefully thanked these colleagues and friends without individually noting their contributions in previous publications. They were regularly thanked on these previous occasions as I expressed gratitude to the faculty at my academic home, the African-American church's largest seminary, the Interdenominational Theological Center. They and all others whom I now mention have one important commonality in addition to the gift of friendship they have shared with me. Every one of these friends has displayed an interest and skill in relating matters of faith to the things of the real world, the very modus operandi of this book.

I start with my colleague in church history, and my mentor in the Black church's history, Kenneth Henry. You do not do history about that tradition without careful attention to how its story has been affected by and has made an impact on American life. Our colleague Melva Costen, eminent liturgical scholar, does much the same with her discipline and special expertise, African-American worship, that Ken does with his. Her husband, James Costen, former president of the seminary I serve, first brought me into the service of the Black church. Thus he and the Center's denominational deans and other officers who keep the school running through their most competent administrative skills hold very special places in my heart as wonderful and supportive friends. What I have said of the work of Melva Costen also pertains to that of Anne Wimberly in Christian education and that of her husband, Edward Wimberly, our academic dean, in pastoral counseling. Both are always asking and writing prodigiously about what their disciplines have to offer the African-American community in light of social realities such as racism. With colleagues like the ones with whom I work, how could I avoid writing a book like this, which tries to relate my own historical investigations to contemporary realities?

Even before I came to the remarkable institution that this son of Norwegian immigrants is privileged to serve, I was inspired by former senior colleagues who have also functioned as models for relating faith to everyday realities. Like my present colleagues, the longtime friends whom I now thank have also been mentors, older scholars who took me under their wings. Two have gone to be with the Lord, but their wonderful spouses, who gently mothered my wife Betsey and me at times we needed it, can still read these words of heartfelt thanks. Dorris Flesner did in his discipline of American Lutheran history what my friend Ken Henry does with the history of the Black church. George Bass, distinguished preaching professor, always modeled how to relate faith to daily life. And then there is Per Lønning, probably Norway's leading living theologian, who managed to combine his distinguished scholarly career with another one in politics (as member of the Norwegian Storting) while still serving as a bishop in the state church. If you want a model for relating faith to contemporary social trends, get to know Per and his work.

Of course, I learned how to relate the traditions of faith to the sociopolitical realities of the day from other Norwegians before I ever met Per. The Ellingsen-Nilssen extended family table was always, and still is, filled with that sort of talk, along with some good arguments about those subjects and a lot of hugs. Thanks to this wonderful family of mine, I grew up believing that you can and should talk about religion and politics.

Last, but certainly not least, there is another inspiration for this book. I refer to the adult I live with, Betsey Shaw Ellingsen. She has been its inspiration in so many ways. Since we first met over thirty years ago, she has directed and encouraged me to relate my scholarly work, not just my faith, to the affairs of everyday American life. And, good lay theologian that she has become, she frequently teaches me how to make these connections. Since she also does a lot of the editing of my writing, the parts of this book that read well are probably her work. It's pretty obvious, then, why she deserves the thanks you noticed on the dedication page. But this book is not just hers and mine. The whole company of friends and family just mentioned, along with all the loyal sons and daughters of the historic Augustinian tradition described in the book, have led the way.

American Society in the New Century
Whatever Happened to Original Sin?

What could the Christian doctrine of original sin possibly have to say to us about the state of America? How can this seemingly quaint idea that infants are born in sin, that all of humanity is innately selfish, contribute to understanding and correcting present trends in American society? The pessimism or cynicism associated with this Christian belief is certainly not what Americans preoccupied with feeling good about themselves want to hear! And yet it is a set of beliefs embedded in the religious communities of American Christians as well as an essential ingredient of the U.S. Constitution and its realism about human nature. Like Reinhold Niebuhr and Martin Luther King Jr., if not James Madison himself, I say that this is the message America needs to hear.[1] As they noted, America will work better, be more blessed, when we address social dynamics with a healthy dose of cynicism, with caution about the motives of our leaders, media gurus, institutions, and ourselves.

A true paradox is involved in making this point, especially for Christians. There is a place for vigorous Christian witness to be made in American government, a witness supported by the Constitution. But that witness has little to do with, and may even be impeded by, insisting on declarations of God's existence in the Pledge of Allegiance or on coins. These references to God may impede the Christian witness by equating the gospel with narrow national interests (America's "civil religion"). The most effective witness Christians can make has to do with the role they play as realists or healthy cynics, reminding society of human fallibility and the flaws of the latest programs and schemes.

With a few exceptions during the reigns of Bush the elder and his heir, Americans have experienced good times since the Reagan era. For significant segments of the population, the American economy has enhanced wealth. Until recently it has enjoyed the longest period of sustained growth since the 1950s. Fortunes have been made on Wall Street. Women and minorities are gradually breaking glass ceilings or at least making it in the middle class on their own terms. We have long been a society that believes in business and personal freedom, enthusiastically mouthing the rhetoric of individual responsibility. But we now have a mania for these values.

Despite these positive developments, all is not well in American society. In the midst of the prosperity, there is much discomfort, anxiety, loneliness, and poverty. The rich get richer, but the poor and the middle class are not keeping pace. In some sense they are even losing ground.[2] Indeed, the members of the middle class feel the pressure of working harder and for more hours just to maintain themselves. Polls indicate that linked to these anxieties is uncertainty about the new economy and our place in it. These anxieties and the sort of personality characteristics and lifestyle options that have come to dominate in America, because they are required in order to succeed in the new economy, are not making Americans happy. Furthermore, they are not good for society as a whole.[3]

Of course, these poll results and others cited in this book by no means imply that our public policy should be shaped primarily by current attitudes. As we will see, the doctrine of original sin and the American constitutional system warn us to avoid being unduly guided by ever-changing public whims. Thus, here and elsewhere my use of poll data is purely for descriptive purposes, merely intended to identify actual behaviors and attitudes of the American public, not to suggest what we should be like.

The anxiety reflected in recent poll results, like anxiety in general, isolates individuals. But an economy such as ours, which demands flexibility, mobility, and superficial levels of cooperation, also isolates individuals. Personal advancement and short-term people skills have come to be valued more than loyalty, quality, and long-term friendships.

Such flexibility occasions the diminution of loyalty and trust with regard not just to fellow human beings but also to institutions, which in time leads them to become irrelevant. For example, Americans today may complain about government, but ultimately most do not care about its institutions and their improvement. Witness the typically small voter turnouts and the dismal statistics regarding knowledge of the Constitution (many Americans were surprised to learn in the 2000 election that the popular vote does not determine the winner of the presidency). Ultimately, government is not perceived as having much effect on people's lives.

The same perceived irrelevance of institutions is evident with regard to education and religion. The home-school movement is a good indication that for many Americans the public school system does not matter. Likewise, modern American pastors are regularly informed that their members do not need the church, that their relationship with God can get along quite nicely without it. Disgruntled church members think nothing of looking elsewhere for a new congregation. Americans may remain connected to the institutions of society, but these institutions no longer have a binding authority. Their members tend to perceive themselves as participating in them by choice. When membership in any group or society is perceived that way, people never unequivocally commit themselves to it, for in principle they can always envisage themselves apart from such a group.

When human beings become isolated from institutions and their history, they turn inward, preoccupied with self-fulfillment and the intensity of their feelings. Social analysts such as Christopher Lasch and, more recently, John Miller have referred to such a lifestyle and the social dynamics associated with it as "narcissism."[4] The impact on American life of the sort of world-view and way of life that the term *narcissism* intends to portray has reached epidemic proportions. "Me-ism" and self-fulfillment are the order of the day. Many Americans are more concerned about their own self-esteem and immediate gratification than about the common good, and about civility and enduring commitments.

Along with the computer and genetic revolutions, new ways of thinking fuel many of these narcissist dynamics. Most of them are related to the German Enlightenment's optimistic view of human nature, a belief that people's judgments, when made rationally and authentically on their own behalf, will always be in their own best interests. This set of assumptions, coupled with a relativism that has reduced values to a matter of personal preference, has come to dominate in contemporary American society. These optimistic, relativistic ways of thinking became the avant-garde worldview of American higher education after the World Wars, and it was only a matter of time before they came to dominate the American social psyche. The impact of this set of beliefs has largely silenced the Constitution's more cynical or realistic view of human nature, as espoused by James Madison through the influence of St. Augustine.[5] The silencing of the Augustinian way of looking at reality has been detrimental to the American way of life. Without the realism it provided, expectations about what individuals deserve and can achieve have been raised so high that we have become a society preoccupied with self-seeking individualism, all to our detriment and higher levels of discontent.

Narcissism and Modern America's Therapeutic Ethos

Sigmund Freud's psychological insights became the cutting edge of American university life only in the middle of the twentieth century. Today a therapeutic vision rooted in a popularized, optimistic version of his insights, especially filtered through the optimism of his rival Carl Jung, permeates every facet of American life.[6] Everywhere, we hear the therapeutic rhetoric of self-fulfillment, "finding yourself," "getting in touch with your feelings," "clarifying your values," "meeting your needs," of self-esteem, repression, defense mechanisms, identity crisis, burnout (in the sense of a dearth of psychic energy), and even of penis envy.

The therapeutic model is increasingly reflected in the judicial system. More and more, crime and our problems are cast in the therapeutic jargon of being "dysfunctional."[7] Think of it: Being psychologically healthy, whole, or true to yourself has a lot more importance for many Americans, at least in today's politically correct discourse, than do professional accomplishments and living out one's religious or ethical commitments. Such accomplishments and commitments must always be seen to serve psychic (mental/emotional) health or else they are likely to be dismissed as "unhealthy behaviors."

Allan Bloom has convincingly explained how the time was ripe for the popularization of these insights.[8] The final years of World War II and those following its conclusion were an era when the social sciences, whose origins were largely German, came to play more profound roles in the curricula of American universities. They tended to assume the role that philosophy departments had previously played. For in this period, philosophy became caught up in an approach called Linguistic Analysis, which tends to bracket speculative questions about worldviews, politics, and ethics in favor of a narrow concentration on analyzing the force or meaning of linguistic assertions. This was not very appealing to the generation that had fought the war or supported the war effort, defeating Nazism's evil empire and benefiting from New Deal collectivism. Its members were naturally more interested in visions of how to bring the benefits of democracy to everyone (which the social sciences seemed to offer) than they were in focusing on the minutiae preoccupying most philosophers of the era.

Other factors led to the widespread popularization of Freud's therapeutic insights. What was avant-garde in the university was in this (not yet anti-intellectualist) era to be something the media elites wanted for themselves. Thus, receiving counseling became chic in Hollywood almost at the same time that the movie industry and television came to have an unprecedented impact on the American social psyche.

Another factor in the impact that the social sciences—and psychology in particular—have had on America since World War II was the nature of the generation that fought the war. This significant group of Americans had not only been weaned on the hardship of the Depression and the need for families and communities to pull together in order to survive but had also been tested by the war (another experience that entailed prioritizing the common good over one's own needs). After the experience of that much self-denial, indulging oneself, one's fantasies, and one's desires seemed rather attractive to some members of that generation—not to mention the generation of those too young to fight, who naturally did not want to be exactly like the war heroes. When the baby-boom children of the heroes came to maturity in the 1960s, it was no surprise that they and generations following them wholeheartedly endorsed the growing cultural consensus on the therapeutic worldview. After all, some of these Boomers had been raised by parents who, though team players themselves, were determined to nurture in their young a sense of their uniqueness. The popularity of Dr. Benjamin Spock and his methods of child-rearing contributed to these dynamics. Psychology's preoccupation with getting in touch with one's feelings and its focus on the individual's self-development also attracted those Baby Boomers rebelling against the team-playing ethos of Mom and Dad. Given these factors, it is understandable that an estimated 30 million Americans living today have sought professional counseling in search of self-fulfillment.

Of course to be in therapy is different from the popularization of therapeutic insights. By the 1960s, if not by the late 1950s, the popularization of these insights had occurred as the therapeutic mindset had become firmly installed in American thinking. The therapist's call to "turn inward" to examine the subconscious world of feelings and fantasies naturally meshed with postwar social dynamics that have fostered our present cultural narcissism. The therapeutic culture fosters narcissism in the sense of counseling or encouraging individuals to express their feelings, to find contentment through expression of those feelings, and not to let anything—even values and binding commitments—get in the way. For the narcissistic lifestyle involves blurring the boundaries between self and world, so that people and life's tasks lose their own independent value and become nothing more than vehicles for the individual's gratification. Therapists and our therapeutic ethos likewise support this dynamic by counseling individuals to put their psychic needs ahead of externals (e.g., values, other people, binding commitments).

The value system of our current American ethos and its narcissistic propensities certainly has affinities to good old selfishness, but other dynamics are involved. Attention to some of the characteristics of clinical narcissism reveals those dynamics.[9] Of course this reflection on clinical narcissism does not intend to imply that most Americans are narcissistic by this clinical definition. Not all Americans are clinically narcissistic in the sense of being enmeshed in the pathological behavior and emotions of the narcissist caught up in rage and pain occasioned by separation trauma in the maturing process. My point is simply to allude to the clinical definition insofar as it converges with our general public mood and attitudes in order better to understand our present social dynamics.

Just as those diagnosed as narcissistic in therapy, people caught up in the narcissistic dynamics of American society are not so preoccupied with self, so turned inward, as to be socially maladroit. Indeed, such persons are often socially ingratiating. After all, relationships are ultimately about giving ego satisfaction, about creating an admiring audience for furthering one's status as celebrity (one who has made it). This sort of interpersonal style fits nicely in the contemporary workplace. In that context, a great premium is now placed on the ability to read relationships, to cultivate networks of support often made up of well-placed admirers, and to easily manage impressions (images) other people have of oneself. The latter two skills mandate a flexibility to do and say most anything without antagonizing others.

The narcissist's world is ultimately about only the self. While the point of this book is to show that selfishness is the human condition, narcissism arises when inhibitions against such selfishness are annulled, when the vision of something more than the self as an ideal is lost. All human beings fall prey to such a way of looking at the world from time to time. What is new is that American society is now sanctioning such a lifestyle, as social and political inhibitions against selfishness have progressively declined. But with the full-scale ascent of narcissism, a bitter irony is clear. Narcissists are left with an inner void in their lives, since ultimately all that populates one's world is the self and its needs. This is a lonely world. The narcissist's devaluation of others entails a lack of curiosity about what he or she encounters. Thus, although frequently extolling the need for formal education and often carrying an inflated estimate of their own intellectual abilities, narcissists lack any real intellectual engagement with the world. As a result, such people never really learn sublimation, which means that they almost compulsively require constant infusions of approval and admiration from others. Without the personality skills to find contentment when immediate yearnings are unfulfilled, the narcissist's only recourse is to depend, in desperation, on the affirmation of others for gratification. Thus the narcissist yearns for celebrity.

So badly needing interaction with people for acclaim, narcissists are even further isolated by their failure ever to get sufficient acclaim to satisfy their too-fragile egos. Such narcissists need other people more desperately than do those with personality types with sound psychological rooting. Yet their preoccupation with self never allows for the development of relationships that are transformative and would lead to emotional interdependence. Consequently, relationships formed by people with the narcissistic personality are manipulative, exploitative, bland, and superficial over any length of time, regardless of their initial intensity. In short, they are unsatisfying. Nothing can last too long or intensely, for as soon as the narcissist's ego fails to receive the instant gratification it so desperately requires, the relationship loses its purpose and must be terminated.

The essential loneliness that narcissists experience at an emotional level typically leads them to chronic boredom with life. To overcome such boredom, they will do what it takes to gain emotional titillation. They will characteristically, even passionately, seek to do the new and interesting but will ultimately fail, because their psychic defenses prevent true intimacy and emotional involvement with the other. Narcissists, then, are promiscuous, in both the sexual and nonsexual senses of the term. They will flit from one thing to the next, finding something new to do as soon as their latest "passion" becomes "boring," which it always does after a couple of months, weeks, or even days.

These traits of the narcissist guarantee that those caught up in this lifestyle can never really find happiness and fulfillment, no matter how talented and important they tell everyone that they are, and no matter how many admirers they manage to accrue for themselves. They remain isolated from everyone and everything around them, even in the midst of their busy social lives, because all these activities and persons are perceived subconsciously as nothing more than (temporary and unstable) extensions of who they are.

This sense of isolation traps narcissists in the present moment. It is only in the present that a person can feel the "high" of having one's ego fed. Such a lifestyle is so flexible in its quest for admiration that it is bound by neither the past nor the future. In fact, who a person was in the past may be a barrier in the quest for instant gratification in the present moment, requiring reinvention of the self. An image change is often regarded as advisable in order to get the job done. Madonna, Michael Jackson, and Bill Clinton are cultural icons who have done this frequently and with flair. Flexibility is the name of the game. Given these dynamics, it is little wonder that more and more Americans are ignorant of and disinterested in history. Likewise, the increasing sense that ours is not a child-friendly society (as nearly 20 percent of America's children are in poverty) bespeaks the narcissistic lack of concern about the future.[10]

Other Social Supports for Narcissism: Consumerism, the Media, American Meritocracy, Contemporary Suburban Living

It needs to be reiterated that the therapeutic ethos that has saturated contemporary American society is not the sole or even the primary cause of the emergence of the narcissist lifestyle on American soil. Consumerism, fostered by the economic expansion since World War II, has also contributed to our narcissist climate. The whole dynamic involved in "growing" the economy is to cultivate needs for new products among the masses. The bottom line of American industries and other businesses during most of the 1990s indicates how successful they have been in this endeavor.

Americans are great shoppers. With all the malls, shopping centers, outlets, and home shopping networks (such as QVC), shopping has become the favorite American pastime. Witness how the malls have become the community centers of suburbia, the place where the teenagers hang out. Besides, shopping helps kill the boredom that narcissists daily experience.

Americans flock to these sites because, among other reasons, the marketing divisions of the corporations have done such a good job. No longer do the advertisements simply call attention to a product and extol it. Advertising in modern America aims to target consumers with a message that they are bored, restless, or unsatisfied with their present realities and holdings. It "educates" the masses into an unappeasable appetite, not only for goods but also for new experiences and personal fulfillment. It presents consumption as the answer to loneliness, boredom, a lack of fulfillment in one's life.[11] Advertisements for Viagra, Slim-Fast, Toyota cars, and L'Oréal's Superior Preference are prime examples. Tide even was advertised in the summer of 2001 as somehow able to improve a stepmother's relationship with her stepdaughter.

Such marketing's negative impact on the social fiber, the role it plays in heightening narcissist outlooks, is obvious. Besides exacerbating the self-fulfillment agenda, modern advertising teaches the public to be discontent with the ordinary. It inspires a sense of limitless cravings typical of narcissism. In so doing, it nurtures new anxieties and insecurities, as consumers are led to reflect on whether they are beautiful, interesting, intelligent, and popular enough.

Another socially problematic outcome of consumerism is that its inherent individualism feeds the narcissist neglect of society's responsibilities to the poor and oppressed. A culture of consumption can function to pacify sentiments of protest or rebellion. The exploitation of the labor force, which is the essence of capitalism (for owners of the capital need to get more from the workers than was invested in them, or there would be no profit), is hidden from workers if when they get home from a hard day on the job they can revel in immediate surroundings full of the latest gadgets.[12]

Other dynamics associated with the American economy have promoted a narcissistic way of perceiving reality. The success of advertising is evident in the data that reveal that Americans are living beyond their means, buying what they cannot afford. That is evident in the double-figure increase in consumer debt in the 1990s.[13] The narcissistic predisposition to live for today is what these statistics proclaim. In that connection, the narcissistic preoccupation with personal fulfillment over all other agendas seems implied by the fact that despite all of America's social challenges throughout the past decade, until recently Gallup poll results indicated that the most important American problem was perceived as the economy. (The reasons that a 2001 poll showed a subordination of this concern to ethics, morality, religion, and family are discussed in chapter 7.)[14]

The nature of post–Industrial Revolution capitalism cannot be overlooked in our investigation of factors making narcissism possible. The factory and today's office separate workers' private world from the public spheres in a way not typical of agrarian (farm-based) economies. And with the less satisfying work that the assembly line and today's office afford, choking off opportunity to be oneself on the job, it is only away from the job that one can really be oneself. Uncertain of who the true self is, since almost as many waking hours are spent being the "other" (public self) on the job, today's working men and women, if they are not too "burned out," are inclined to "go for all the gusto" they can in each private moment, to seek fulfillment in any way possible. Uncertain about who they are, though, they may try to fill the empty gaps with more commodities. The American (Western) labor system helps nurture narcissism, as well as better consumers.

New dimensions of the American economy are no less prone to encouraging the narcissist lifestyle. The advent of cable TV and the new computer ethos, especially the Internet, further feeds the narcissist dynamics of contemporary American society. Both of these media flood consumers with choices and opportunities for sensual titillation. (Think of the virtual realities the computer makes available.) When you have that many choices, opportunities to practice loyalty become rarer and rarer. And people without a sense of loyalty are, in the fashion of narcissism, more likely to favor the quest for self-fulfillment over binding commitments when push comes to shove. Likewise a public regularly exposed to a flood of exciting, titillating experience is more likely going to experience narcissist boredom in "real-life" moments away from the computer and the tube. When regularly exposed to the sensational and the exciting, then like the addicts that we so easily become, human beings crave more excitements and sensationalism.

The reference to addiction in describing the narcissist way of life is not accidental. Emptiness, boredom, and craving for titillation lead a narcissist culture to seek "highs" and "meaning" by any means possible. Drugs provide those. Little wonder many Americans are drugged up (or at least experimenting).

Another related implication of electronic media is their role in nurturing a lifestyle of instant gratification, short attention spans, flexibility, feeling or passion over thought, and so the promotion of simple answers and images to complex problems. Cerebral, complex solutions to problems and old-fashioned values do not play well. Part of the problem is the very nature of the media. Television and the movies are action media. Their stories always involve dissection. They can never present the whole picture and are rarely able to provide historical or cultural background. In addition, the media's stress on action (the need for ratings) biases them toward the sensational—the unusual, the bizarre, and the illegal. Because of this, much of life—its usual, most beautiful dimensions—does not get air time.[15]

The electronic media's infatuation with the sensational and bizarre is evident not just in their inherent characteristics but, especially in recent decades, in the content and lifestyles displayed on the tube and on the big screen. Movies began to change in 1966 when the Motion Picture Association junked the old Hays Production Code, which since 1930 had imposed restrictions on movie makers concerning obscene language, sex, violence, religious ridicule, ethnic insults, and drug abuse. Plenty of examples can be cited of the consequences of these actions. More recently, gratuitous violence and aberrant sex have been displayed in *American Pie* and its sequel, and in *Kids and Bullies*. In *Scary Movie* and *Scary Movie 2*, semen hits a ceiling. The American public has sensed that boundaries are being violated—though not much, given recorded movie attendance levels. Nevertheless, in 1991, a Gallup poll found that nearly seven of ten Americans blamed the movies to some extent for causing violence in society.

Television and the contemporary music industry are no less infatuated with the values and behavior of narcissistic, even nihilistic, lifestyles. A recent (summer 2001) study by the Parents Television Council indicated that more episodes of violence and coarse language appeared in the 2000–2001 television season during early prime time (the so-called family viewing hours) than were identified in a 1998–1999 study. The Family Research Council, reporting on a recent television season, observed that of all the sex we see or hear about on the tube, unmarried partners are engaged in it five times more than are married couples.[16] *Sex in the City* and MTV offerings like *Spring Break* are especially good illustrations of this phenomenon. For pure sleaze, there is the *Jerry Springer Show*, with uplifting pieces on children who sleep with their mothers and practitioners of spouse-swapping. As for music, most rap features narcissistic lifestyles. Eminem is the king, with his graphically sexual lyrics, and Missy Elliott sings of getting your "freak on" (having sex, in African-American slang).

A no less unattractive feature of all these media is their tendency to nurture a dilettante way of life (something like what Søren Kierkegaard called the aesthetic stage). We become "spectators" of the most intimate details of fellow humans, experiencing "intimacy" without vulnerability and commitment.[17]

To be sure, the Internet and cable TV are not the cause of our narcissist ethos. But in a climate in which other dynamics have ineluctably occasioned narcissist perspectives in segments of the population and work to develop these traits in all of us, these new media efficaciously contribute to the narcissist ethos.

Elite opinion makers in American society who have sought to encourage personal responsibility have unwittingly enhanced narcissistic ways of thinking. Especially in the Clinton era, the idea that America had fulfilled the democratic idea by establishing a meritocracy became widespread in elite sociopolitical circles.[18] This is the idea that those who reach the top and prosper are those who have earned it by their ability and hard work.

Individualism and the therapeutic model of reality are obviously implicit in such a vision of the way things work in America. The vision certainly makes those at the top feel good about themselves. Of course it also helps them forget about the indebtedness they have to others, for a meritocracy is likely to foster the belief among those who succeed that their success is the result of their own achievement; they forget that those who achieve usually have at least the benefit of a superior education, if not other advantages of affluence. If you did not get that advantageous head start, you will probably not "merit" a life of success in the American meritocracy.

The mindset associated with understanding the contemporary American system as a meritocracy leads to two apparently different but still compatible reactions in the new socioeconomic system. On the one hand, the winners will forget the underclass who remain in poverty, on the false grounds that the underclass had the same opportunities as the winners. This dynamic helps explain why so many Baby Boomers who supported Johnson's Great Society ideals in the 1960s—and the concern for the poor implicit in these programs—vote Republican and bash the poor today.

Another reaction is that losers emerge and feel terribly guilty or unhappy about their failure to succeed. (In less mobile societies the underclass do not experience such a sense of failure, for they know they never had a chance.) Through contact with the losers, the specter of failure always clouds the lives of winners in a meritocracy with the fear that they too could still lose.[19] As a result, both the winners and the losers in today's meritocracy (the underclass, without prestigious college degrees, never got in the game) are typically ensconced in the therapeutic mindset. In part this is a function of needing to protect themselves or their self-esteem, since believers in meritocracy have eliminated most of the sociological excuses for failure.[20]

There is a chicken-and-egg relationship between our present socioeconomic environment and the narcissistic outlook on life. It is not easy to discern which really occasions the other. Each impacts and supports the other.

For example, just as narcissism is fostered by contemporary economic developments, so the narcissistic preoccupation with self-fulfillment in turn helps explain our present pro-business climate. When people are preoccupied with themselves, finding ways to make money and accumulate power so that they can be admired is more likely to attract them than are opportunities for quiet and unglamorous humanitarian service. Thus, even the professions that continue to attract—medicine and law—do so primarily because of the high wages and the way in which these professions are now related to the world of big business. Law and medicine make significant profits by serving big business. And both the legal corporation and the health maintenance organization have adopted business models in dispensing their services.[21]

The suburban life of middle-class and upper-middle-class Americans also supports a narcissistic way of life. In the American subdivision, we can avoid meeting our neighbors if we choose, and so preserve our privacy. Neighbors do not typically share common meeting places, as they did in the small town, the urban neighborhood, and even the suburbs of the 1950s. The people we see in the mall are transients, as we are. There is no permanence. When we do encounter our neighbors and get to know them, it does not happen involuntarily, but by choice. We are in charge of who we know and associate with in the neighborhood. The sets of relationships are more homogeneous, since, unlike in the small town or the city, the people in our subdivisions are like ourselves, with a socioeconomic and often an ethnic and racial background like our own. These encounters are also, more often than not, age-segregated. As a result, children and adolescents are more segregated today, for they are usually set aside in their own space—adolescents in their teen-culture happenings and children in day-care activities—always with adults endeavoring to supervise educational activities in these territories. Consequently, they have less and less opportunity to improvise a social life of their own by appropriating adult activities through the emulation that comes from observing and participating in such adult activities. If we lament that kids no longer organize themselves in their own activities, it may be because in the new suburbia they do not see adults doing it for themselves. Besides, adults do much of the organizing of kids' activities for them.[22]

All of these dynamics contribute to a narcissistic ethos. As our interactions in the community are only by choice and are homogeneous, the narcissist-like specter of the other as a mere extension of who I am is reinforced. Children, whose primary interaction with adults is in day care or in "quality time" in which parents try to assuage their guilt by giving their children a memorable moment, likewise get this narcissistic message.

How Narcissistic Are We?

The impact of narcissistic ways of thinking on society is evident in American views on sex and family. Again, the relationship is chicken-and-egg in character, insofar as the new attitudes and behaviors related to sex and marriage also support the narcissistic way of life. A May 2001 Gallup poll certainly supports this thesis. It revealed that while in 1961 only 21 percent of the American public believed that premarital sex was morally acceptable, forty years later 52 percent of the public accept the morality of such behavior. Such attitudes seem borne out statistically in census data: since 1990 there has been a 71.77 percent rise in the number of cohabiting unmarried heterosexual couples.

Part of this dynamic is related to the fact that marriage has fallen on hard times, and to some extent the increase in cohabitation may reflect the divorce epidemic. There is no question that marriages do not last like they did in the 1950s. While there has been a decline in the divorce rate since it hit its peak in 1981, the most recent nationwide count in 1996 revealed that there has been a fivefold increase in the number of divorces since 1950, a marked rise even when population growth is taken into account (from 2.6 per 1,000 people in 1950 to 4.3 per 1,000 in 1996). In the same period the number of marriages dropped by almost 20 percent.[23] It is evident that the narcissistic preference for short-term, self-fulfilling relationships is gaining headway over lifelong commitments.

The short-term, live-for-today, forget-the-future narcissistic viewpoint has also manifested itself in American personal finances. Pressured by their narcissistic drive for instant gratification and the sophisticated marketing of today's businesses, Americans borrowed more for consumer spending by a double-figure increase in the 1990s. Metropolitan Life has estimated that younger Baby Boomers have amassed personal debt equal to a startling 95 percent of their annual income. The *Wall Street Journal* reported that household levels of debt rose from 1995 through 1999 by a record level of $6.3 trillion, so that the percentage of after-tax income was only 1.5 percent.[24]

I hasten to note that I am not claiming that every American is caught up in the narcissist lifestyle, or even that the majority of Americans are living in this mode. However, as noted, it cannot be denied that elements of this lifestyle are portrayed in the media as glamorous, as the lifestyle of celebrity. Nor can we overlook how the therapeutic, pro-business ethos that dominates present American life lends support to, even implicitly encourages, certain narcissistic modes of being in the world. Consequently, even those not sucked into the narcissistic way of life, typical middle-class Americans still living in "traditional family" arrangements, providing for their children's futures, and actively participating in community religious organizations, will nevertheless be pressured to conform to the narcissistic way of being. At the very least this manifests in a tendency to interpret their very traditional way of life in therapeutic, narcissistic categories, not unlike the way in which immigrants and minorities in America have been pressured to conform to the "American way."

The problem is even more intense for ethnic minorities. They are exposed to the same pressures as the White upper-middle classes. The media are as effective in marketing their messages to them as to the majority and the privileged classes. But the yearnings and despair that accompany the narcissistic lifestyle are intensified for them by an economic and social system that still effectively marginalizes them, robs them of the glimmer of hope that they might achieve the celebrity lifestyle promulgated by the media. (To African Americans, the media message has tended to be that their only hope for celebrity is in professional sports or music, so they mustn't even dream about anything else.) In addition to encountering narcissistic boredom and emptiness, racial minorities and, to a lesser extent, the systemically impoverished of all ethnic groups experience a cultural ethos that communicates to them a feeling that they are inherently inferior.

In a narcissistic ethos where, without any sense of guilt, people use people to meet their own needs, there is little likelihood that efforts will be made by those with power to eradicate poverty and racism. Indeed, keeping such folk in "their place" ensures that an audience will envy the celebrity, and such celebrity status is precisely what the narcissist craves. The growth of the impoverished class (the poorest of the poor, making under $14,000 annually) and the new racism's emergence since the Reagan years make despicably perfect sense in a narcissist culture.

The Root Cause of Our Social Ills and the Antidote

The question with which this introduction began has been answered by being ignored. Most readers already have a sense that the Christian view of original sin simply has no place in contemporary American social trends. A 2000 *New York Times* poll confirmed this: 73 percent of the respondents claimed that people are born good, and 85 percent thought that they could be pretty much anything they wanted to be.[25] Besides interfering with this consensus about American optimism, the Christian view of original sin gets in the way of narcissistic dynamics, and it certainly conflicts with the pro-business, therapeutic ethos that dominates social life today. There are historical reasons as well as logical reasons for the neglect of original sin by today's Americans.

It is true that there are precedents for the neglect of original sin and of an appreciation of the degree to which all human beings are plagued by an insidious egocentricity. We will note in the second chapter the intellectual influences on the founding fathers that worked to silence this vision of reality. Significantly, these influences emerged from certain secular strands of the Enlightenment (the eighteenth- and nineteenth-century era characterized by a spirit of rationalism and empiricism that was militantly skeptical of any authoritative claims to truth made by traditional institutions but not authorized by either reason or experience). However, it is the more recent post–World War trends that have had the most success in silencing this pessimistic, realistic way of thinking.

This raises the question of why the post–World War trends have silenced the more realistic earlier (even constitutionally rooted) way of thinking. In a sense, the answer is identical with the answer to the question about the root cause of all our social ills. Once again, history tells the story.

It is no accident that the discipline of psychology that has nurtured our narcissism, as well as much modern science and technology, is rooted in the intellectual climate of the German or English Enlightenment. This is significant for understanding why the biblical and constitutional view of the flawed, sinful nature of human beings has fallen on hard times in contemporary America. The Enlightenment, the mother of psychology and its related dynamics, presupposed a very optimistic view of human nature. Most of its premier spokespersons emphasized ethics and posited the ability of human beings to do good unaided by divine intervention.[26] The ethos of meritocracy and of the role of choice that modern denizens of suburbia make in establishing relationships likewise presupposes Enlightenment conceptions of unbridled freedom, which itself entails that humans are essentially good or capable of doing good.

This brings us to how the Christian doctrine of original sin, with its realistic vision of human nature, is needed to counteract the negative trends we have been noting. I refer here to the doctrine as it was originally conceived for Christendom by the great early African Christian thinker, St. Augustine (354–430). As will be noted subsequently in more detail, not everything that passes for the doctrine of original sin in Christian circles is in fact in harmony with and as realistic as this classical Augustinian formulation. To the degree that narcissism, the therapeutic ethos, and related problems are functions of the optimism of Americans regarding human capabilities, the way to deal with many of these social ills is to achieve a widespread social consensus among Americans that we are not as good as we think. This book will show, paradoxically, that when we realize our limits and our insidious motives, we are more likely to be tolerant of our neighbors' agendas, and more likely to get in the trenches and work to make things better, more likely to appreciate ourselves and the direction of our nation. The more the doctrine of original sin permeates our thinking, the better (though by no means perfect) life in America is likely to be.

one

The Augustinian Understanding
of Reality

We need to clarify the Augustinian doctrine of sin, not just for the sake of society, but for the sake of the church. The doctrine is one of the most misinterpreted Christian commitments. Even in the church at the turn of the millennium, the doctrine as originally formulated by St. Augustine has fallen on hard times.

In our present therapeutic/narcissist ethos, most Americans are likely to hear the phrase *original sin* and smile uneasily. The whole idea is rather quaint, cultural gurus assert. People are not born evil as a result of the sexual origins of human life. We are self-made human beings, society contends. We determine our own fate; we must take responsibility for the good and evil we do and not make excuses with a crutch like original sin. Perhaps we make our mistakes, but surely we can do some good things, we insist. Besides, society contends (saturated as it is by therapeutic jargon), we need to affirm human capacities and not be so negative.

Many pastors of different denominations report a similar reaction to their sermons these days. If they refer several times to human sinfulness or if they condemn sin, someone is likely to say they do it all the time and then chide them for being too negative, for failing to build their congregation up. The church is as heavily ensconced in the therapeutic cultural ethos and its optimistic view of human nature as is American society as a whole. Salvation and the healthy spiritual life are about psychologically healthy existence, life without guilt. We are told that people unburdened of such negativity will do the right thing.

All of these contentions, in both the contemporary church and in American society, bespeak the kind of optimism and therapeutic preoccupations we have already identified in today's prevailing social trends. They also suggest precisely the same worldview that led Augustine to formulate the doctrine of original sin: the heresy of the English monk Pelagius.

Augustinian and Pre-Augustinian Roots

Although St. Augustine was the one to formulate the doctrine of original sin as it eventually became codified as official church teaching at the Council of Ephesus in 431 and again at the Synod of Orange in 529, there were significant early precedents for the doctrine. The first monks, who populated African deserts, had strong doctrines of sin. St. Anthony (ca. 251–356), the most famous of these monks, is a prime example. He combined this commitment, though, with an affirmation of free will.[1] His colleagues in the desert were more radical in speaking of the hold sin has on us. Longinus and Matoes spoke of sin in terms of passions that overcome the soul. Moses the Negro found another image to describe the sins that gripped him, noting that "sins run behind me, and I do not see them. . . ." Earlier in the third century, a bishop in North Africa, Commodianus, had even identified sin with desire.[2]

The great champion of trinitarian doctrine, Athanasius (ca. 296–373), bishop of Alexandria, an older contemporary of Augustine who was himself a devoted advocate of the monks, continued in their tradition regarding the seriousness with which he took human sin. He spoke of the corruption caused by sin, how because of it the human race was perishing and the image of God disappearing in human beings as they became clouded by demoniacal deceit and insatiable in sinning. Like the monks, though, Athanasius still affirmed human free will.[3]

Earlier eminent theologians made comments suggestive of the doctrine of original sin. Tertullian (ca. 160–225) referred to Adam as "the originator of our race and our sin." Cyprian of Carthage (200–258) subsequently made affirmations about baptism that were also directly pertinent to the development of the doctrine of original sin. In justifying the practice of infant baptism, he referred to the sin of infants in the sense of their having been "born of the flesh according to Adam," contracting "the contagion of the ancient death."[4] These early thinkers of the church clearly laid the groundwork for understanding sin as something that is bigger than us and our misdeeds, as a reality or condition that infects our entire nature, even from birth.

Of course there were biblical precedents for these affirmations. The Old Testament has many express references to "sins" against the commandments and law of God, and the Gospels continued to refer to sins in this tradition. One notes at an early stage in the development of these Old Testament texts that sin came to be related not just to misdeeds but also to a lack of faith (Exodus 32, esp. v. 21).

The Genesis 3 account of the Fall of Adam and Eve became a crucial text for the Christian doctrine of sin. Although Jewish leaders did not understand the Fall in this way, New Testament writers began to speak of the transmission of sin to all humanity through Adam (Rom. 5:12–14; 1 Cor. 15:22). Psalm 51:5 ("I was . . . a sinner when my mother conceived me") can be cited to support this idea that one is born in sin by virtue of the Fall.

Other texts are pertinent for establishing the pervasive character of sin, that it is more than mere misdeeds and instead a reality that saturates the whole of human nature. Romans 7 (esp. vv. 14–23) portrays sin as a reality that forces human beings to do and to will what they otherwise would not want to do. For our purposes as we seek to identify the social implications of the traditional doctrine of sin, Ecclesiastes 4:4 seems relevant. The text reads: "Then I saw that all labor and all skill in work come from one person's envy of another. This also is vanity and a chasing after wind." The text suggests that every dimension of the work that transpires in society is the result of envy and the desire to get ahead of one's neighbor (i.e., the result of competition and concupiscence).

The occasion for gathering up these insights into a fully developed doctrine of original sin in which all sins are said to be rooted was a famous controversy between Augustine and Pelagius (ca. 360–420), a devout monk from Britain (perhaps Ireland). Famous for his piety and austerity, Pelagius despaired over the lackluster Christianity that seemed to plague his era. His response was to teach and preach a rigid moralism. Christian life was to be viewed as an effort to overcome sins and attain salvation. This required a belief that people have complete freedom to sin or not to sin.

Pelagius's debate with Augustine was touched off by Augustine's prayer in his classic work *The Confessions:* "Give what Thou command and command what Thou wilt." Pelagius rejected the idea that God commands the impossible, as Augustine seemed to imply.[5] The two contemporaries would be locked in a heated debate for years to come, with Augustine's side eventually prevailing. Had it not prevailed, it is likely we would never have heard of the doctrine of original sin. The church (and the U.S. Constitution) would have been very different.

Augustine's primary agenda was not to lament the power of sin but to assert the primacy of God's action and forgiving love, to confess that the Lord Jesus Christ is humanity's only hope. Pelagius's vision of how we are saved contradicted that. If we are not totally immersed in sin, then it logically follows that we can save ourselves, that we do not need Christ. The testimony of Mark 2:7 that God alone can forgive sins, and that only Jesus has been able to exercise that authority, seems to be at stake in these commitments.

In addition to these commitments, Augustine's own life had revealed to him the hopelessness of the human condition in sin.[6] So bound to sin are we, he insisted (in the spirit of Romans 7), that when it comes to avoiding sin we have no free will.

Without grace, we cannot stop sinning. As he put it: "Free choice alone, if the way of truth is hidden, avails for nothing but sin; and when the right action and true aim has begun to appear clearly, there is still no doing, no devotion, no good life."[7]

If we have free will and can in principle choose the good, we open the door again to the possibility that we can overcome sin and save ourselves. Again, our total dependence on God is at stake in these commitments. (For Christians, certain biblical texts such as Rom. 3:21–28, Gal. 3:1–14, and Eph. 2:8–9 are on the line.) The next time we are tempted to raise questions about the doctrine of sin or want to affirm free will (in the sense of asserting that we have the power to do good without grace), we might keep in mind that in so doing we are effectively minimizing our dependence on God.

Our bondage in sin does not necessarily mean that we are reduced to robots. It is theologically appropriate to continue to assert our freedom to choose actions without compromising the claim that we are in bondage to sin. For example, it might be possible to assert that you, the reader, are free to decide whether to continue reading this book today or whether to discontinue reading. On Augustine's grounds, either way you are sinning, because the decision you make in either case is self-serving (doing what makes you feel good).[8]

The challenge next faced by Augustine was how to unequivocally assert our bondage to sin. The weight of precedent and how the biblical witness had been interpreted in previous centuries moved the African Father to talk about sin as something we are born with and to depict it in terms of desire or lust.[9] Certainly, when we are lusting (be it a sexual lust or a lust for power or things), we are in bondage to that person or thing. You cannot make many free decisions in the heat of passion. You just do what the lust demands.

Augustine described this bondage to lust as concupiscence, designating concupiscence as "the law of sin."[10] *Concupiscence,* of course, is a term referring to a strong, compelling desire, especially like sexual lust. The term had autobiographical significance for Augustine insofar as he had struggled with sexual lust in the course of his spiritual pilgrimage. By employing the term to describe the essence of sin, the African Father was provided with a powerful way of expressing the bondage of sin without reducing fallen humanity to mere robots. Just as in the heat of sexual passion we cannot stop the sexual encounter, so sinners seeking their own gratification cannot stop seeking it, even when they know better. It is as Paul said in Romans 7:15 and 19: "I do not understand my own actions. For I do not do what I want, but I do the very thing I hate. . . . For I do not do the good I want, but the evil I do not want is what I do." Augustine conceives of fallen human beings as addicts. Like sex addicts, the more we are driven to seek pleasure and self-fulfillment, the less we will be satisfied, and so the more pleasures we will need to seek. The more you desire, the more you sin, and the more you sin, the more you desire. The African Father more or less made this point when he claimed that (human) nature and custom (our actions) join together to render cupidity stronger.[11]

It would be a mistake to understand Augustine as defining sin merely as lustful actions that result in visible violations of the Ten Commandments and of the expectations of good citizenship in a society. His point in describing sin as concupiscence was to make clear that *all* human deeds, even the ones outwardly good, are sinful. Augustine did believe sinful human beings are capable of outwardly good deeds. Indeed, such acts are no less outwardly good than deeds motivated by the love of God. He even claimed that the works of pride (concupiscence) are akin to those of love. Both can feed the hungry and care for the dying. The difference is that love does what it does for Christ, while pride does what it does in order that the doer may be glorified.[12]

There is indeed a sense in which, on Augustinian grounds, the behavior of Abraham Lincoln and Martin Luther King Jr. was no better than that of the likes of Hitler or Osama bin Laden. All were driven by lust for power and influence (concupiscence) in some sense. Before God, they and we stand equally condemned unless the miracle of God's forgiving grace intervenes. However, if we speak in terms of relative degrees of human goodness and justice, then of course the actions of Lincoln and King may be judged as better, even as good. Augustine himself made this distinction as he spoke of a "righteousness in the Law," which is mere obedience to its letter, as distinct from the "righteousness of the Law," which only God gives by grace. Some Reformation-era heirs of the African Father offered a similar distinction between the "civic or external righteousness" of the good citizen and the righteousness of God given in justification of the sinner.[13]

Everything that fallen human beings do is ultimately motivated not by the love of God, but by the burning desire to please the ego. Thus Augustine claimed that new desires (concupiscence) are increased and receive greater energies from prohibitions of the Law.[14] When I am urged to do something, to succeed, become powerful, do good, my ego begins to crave these things even more than ever before. As a result, even the good deeds that I do are scarred by my egocentric desires to do good.

The law of God energizes concupiscence in other ways. Prohibitions have a way of causing rebellion, at least of the covert sort. When the boss says "do it my way or else," when someone says you cannot undertake this activity, it is likely you will want to do that forbidden deed even more. In our sinful condition, we never outgrow our childishness. We are like children who are forbidden certain toys or like teenagers wanting more "freedom." The prohibitions of God's law make us want what is forbidden even more.

Augustine found another provocative way to express the insidious character of human behavior after the Fall into sin. He began with the reflection that of all that exists only God can be enjoyed. For only God gives the good and happy life. All other things are there only for use, since they cannot offer the good and happy life. In short, the best we can do in our interactions with the things of the world is use them. Is that true? Ultimately, do we not *use* what we love—our vocations, our friends, even our families— to our own benefit and for our own gratification? Augustine concedes that there is a way of finding true joy in the things of the earth, but only when we enjoy these loves as things or vehicles of God, who alone brings true joy.[15] Even in these cases, though, Christians are still only using the things of the earth, only using the people they love. In using our loved ones as vehicles to find joy, we seem to subordinate them to our own desires and ego. This side of eternity, then, concupiscence never goes away.

These reflections help us understand what a life without concupiscence, a life lived in eternity in the presence of God, is like. It would be a life of enjoyment, not one of using people and things. I do not elaborate much on this point here, since our politics should never be influenced by this eternal vision lest we confuse our politics with the kingdom of God. The elaboration of this vision is a book for another time.[16] At this point, suffice it to say that if we fully enjoy God, then all that surrounds us is enjoyed as stemming from him. In such a state I and all that surrounds me is of God. We share a common gene pool, as it were, a restoration of the common gene pool in which human life began in Eve's womb.[17] Consequently, my desires are no longer concupiscent, just for personal fulfillment, but for the fulfillment of the genes outside me, for my neighbor. It is as good if they succeed as if I do. Although some expressions of human relations may foreshadow this (like the love of parent for child or between spouses), since the Fall into sin, none succeeds in canceling out my prioritizing of my own needs over those of my kin.

Augustine made his point regarding the inescapable character of concupiscence and egocentricity in a way that has been most controversial. However, when we really analyze the point in light of the realities of the sex drive, it seems valid. Essentially, Augustine concluded that we are born into our concupiscence. Following the lead of an earlier North African bishop, Cyprian of Carthage, he maintained that we are concupiscent because we are conceived in concupiscence.[18]

Augustine's point is not to suggest anything so simplistic as that we are conceived in sin, or that sex is sinful. But the reality is that the "very embrace [between spouses] which is lawful and honorable cannot be effected without the ardour of lust." Likewise, the sexual encounter that follows from such foreplay is driven by concupiscence and lust. (If you do not have some of that left in a marital encounter, it may not be a good marriage.) Sometimes the result of this encounter is fertilization of the egg, the beginning of human life. And so God uses human concupiscence to create new life. The product of such human concupiscence is likely to be marked by its concupiscent parental origins, just as we bear our parents' genes. Conceived as the product of concupiscence, it is no wonder we turn out that way.

A distinct twentieth-century version of this way of thinking can be articulated on the basis of the work of the eminent Swiss Reformed theologian Karl Barth. In essence, he maintained the doctrine of original sin, the inevitability of sin, by contending that we are what we do or what is done to us. Human beings do not have static, essential natures. For example, Mark Ellingsen is nothing more than the sum total of all the things that he has done and that have happen to him. Given the Barthian scheme, we can observe that just as Mark Ellingsen and the readers of this volume have been exposed only to concupiscent human beings, except for Jesus Christ, it is hardly surprising that the nature formed by encounter with the world would itself be concupiscent.[19] We can understand Augustine's depiction of original sin in light of Barth's more sociological analysis. Either way, the inevitability of sin, the assertion of how we are marred by sin from birth, is nonnegotiable for the classical Christian doctrine of sin.

Augustine and those who followed him sought to protect these nonnegotiable assertions by insisting that even Christians always remain concupiscent. Concupiscence remains even after one comes to faith and is baptized.[20] If that were not true, Christians would not need Christ and grace as much as they did before conversion.

Many contemporary Christians and even some older denominations (especially Methodist-Holiness churches) have a hard time with this idea. But if Augustine and the classical formulation of the doctrine of original sin are taken seriously, then Christians must concede the insidious egoism of which they cannot rid themselves. Even going to church, partici-

pating in its activities, and preaching a sermon are undertaken for one's own enrichment or (at least in some sub-sub-
cultures and communities) for the acclaim or appreciation
that such activities furnish, as much as they are done for God.
As we shall see, America's founders believed this, and so do
American Christians who do not effectively relegate non-
Christians to the status of second-class citizens. Christians
who do not share these commitments are at least implicitly
claiming to be above the fray that the Constitution was made
to order.

Insofar as it concerns itself with the very essence of what it
means to be human, with the human condition, it is not surprising that the doctrine of sin has implications for understanding society and politics. Augustine himself recognized
that. Thus, in the spirit of Ecclesiastes 4:4, he elaborated on
the logic of his treatment of the doctrine by noting how sin
(concupiscence) permeates every segment of social life:

> We give a much more unlimited approval to their idea that the
> life of the wise man must be social. . . . But who can enumerate
> all the great grievances with which human society abounds in
> the misery of this mortal state? . . . Hear how one of their comic
> writers makes one of his characters express the common feel-
> ings of all men in this matter: "I am married; this is one misery.
> Children are born to me; they are additional cares."

> What shall I say of these judgments which men pronounce on
> men, and which are necessary in communities, whatever out-
> ward peace they enjoy? Melancholy and lamentable judgments
> they are, since the judges are men who cannot discern the con-
> sciences of those at their bar . . .[21]

> Worldly society has flowed from a selfish love. . . . In the city of
> the world both the rulers themselves and the people they dom-
> inated are dominated by the lust for domination. . . . Hence, even
> the wise men in the city of men live according to man, and their
> only goal has been the goods of their bodies or of the mind or
> of both.[22]

Because of our concupiscence, our innate propensity to use people and position for our own benefit, social interactions will always be flawed. As we have noted, no relationship, not even with one's beloved family, will be perfect, free of hassles and heartaches, for even these relationships are marred by power struggles between their members to get their own way. Get real about love. Revel in what's good about what you have, despite the times when one party gets his or her way though manipulation. Christians may even enjoy their imperfect relationships when family and friends are seen as gifts and vehicles of God, and precautions are taken to guard against one-sided dominance of the interests of some in the family over those of the others. Likewise, no institution, even the courts and the legislature, will be unbiased. We need to find ways to minimize the bias as best we can.

These are very important insights for understanding the realities that the writers of the American Constitution tried to address. As such, they are significant insights for trying to understand the present realities of American society.

Whose Augustine? The American Version

I hasten to note that references to Augustine's views in this chapter represent a constructive appropriation of the African Father's thinking, more than a historical-critical analysis. The version of Augustine portrayed is more in line with Protestant appropriations of his thought, which consistently identify concupiscence with sin.[23] In fact, the historical Augustine sometimes rejected the equation of concupiscence with sin, referring to it as merely that which produces sin.[24] However, inasmuch as Protestantism, and particularly Reformation appropriations of Augustine, have had the primary influence on the institutions of the American republic, it seems appropriate to devote primary attention to this version of Augustine's thought.

We can illustrate the last point merely by recalling the profound impact that Puritanism had on the American colonies and the founders. Some historians, notably the eminent American church historian Sydney Ahlstrom, have referred to a Puritan paradigm for understanding American religion and American society as a whole. By that, Ahlstrom and like-minded scholars mean that when the American public thinks of religion, when the opinion makers and the media allude to religion, they interpret or portray it in Puritan categories. Puritan categories underlie religious versions of the American myth (i.e., the idea of America as a chosen people or a blessed nation). Likewise, America's most influential religious traditions, the status churches to which to belong, are typically those with roots in Puritanism (Presbyterian, Baptist, Congregational, Methodist) or which generated Puritanism (the Episcopal Church).[25]

The presence of the Augustinian view of original sin in the religious traditions that shaped America is readily evident. The premier Puritan doctrinal statement, the one adopted by Presbyterians and all the New England Puritan synods, the Westminster Confession, affirms this conception. Article VI of the document refers to our inherited corrupted nature:

> whereby we are utterly indisposed, disabled, and made opposite to all good and wholly inclined to do all evil . . . this corruption of nature, during this life, doth remain in those that are regenerated.

Article VIII proceeds to affirm the reality of bondage to sin, claiming that humankind "hath wholly lost all ability of will to any spiritual good."

Similar commitments are expressed in the authoritative Episcopal doctrinal statement, the Thirty-nine Articles. Article IX affirms the existence of original sin, claiming that

> . . . it is the fault and corruption of the Nature of every man, that naturally is engendered for the offspring of Adam; whereby man is very far gone from original righteousness, and is of his own nature inclined to evil, so that the flesh lusteth always contrary to the Spirit.

The next article also rejects the notion of free will, affirming the reality of human bondage to sin.

The largest Protestant body in the United States, the Southern Baptist Convention, is likewise in touch with these affirmations. Its Baptist Faith and Message document (in Article III) notes that every human being inherits "a nature and an environment inclined toward sin."[26] Even the Quaker heritage, so influential on the American scene in the pre-Revolutionary era, along with Puritanism, maintained commitments compatible with the Augustinian vision. In a 1678 document outlining Quaker beliefs by Robert Barclay, a disciple of Quaker founder George Fox, Proposition IV observed that "All Adam's posterity . . . is fallen, degenerated, dead, deprived of the sensation or feeling of this inward testimony or seed of God. . . ."

But the most direct impact of the Augustinian vision of reality on America was mediated through a great Scottish Presbyterian philosopher, Thomas Reid (1710–1796), whose Common Sense Realist philosophy had a significant impact at the College of New Jersey (now Princeton University), the very undergraduate institution attended by James Madison. On the faculty was a Scottish Presbyterian immigrant to the colonies, a proponent of Common Sense Realism, John Witherspoon (1723–94), who signed the Declaration of Independence and was one of Madison's teachers. First, we turn to the Augustinianism of Reid. Noting how human nature is ever in the quest for self-gratification, he wrote: "To serve God and be useful to mankind, without any concern about our own good and happiness, is, I believe, beyond the pitch of human nature."[27]

Reid's predecessor in the development of Common Sense Realism, Francis Hutcheson (1694–1746), noted critically and emphasized even more strongly that the moral sense is driven by our desires to do what promotes our own needs, giving us maximum pleasure.[28] As for Witherspoon, he wrote an entire treatise entitled, "All Mankind by Nature under Sin." In a speech made to the Continental Congress as the Articles of Confederation were being drafted, he stated: "I am none of those who either deny or conceal the depravity of human nature . . ."[29]

In another treatise on moral philosophy, probably delivered to Princeton students (including Madison) in 1772, Witherspoon elaborated on the political implications of this set of Augustinian commitments. He wrote:

> Every good form of government must be complex . . . so that one principle may check the other. . . . It is folly to expect that a state should be upheld by integrity of all who have a share in managing it. They must be so balanced that when one draws to his own interest or inclination, there may be an over poise upon the whole.[30]

Can the Augustinian Vision Communicate Today?

Some might challenge the apparent pessimism and cynicism of this Augustinian vision of human nature. Readers saturated in the therapeutic climate of contemporary American culture, with its optimism about what humans can do, are likely still to feel ill at ease. The suspicion is that looking at life in the sense of classical Christianity makes you hopeless, undermines your self-respect, and cripples your activism, since you feel that all you do is sin.

The great twentieth-century American Reformed theologian (a member of today's United Church of Christ) Reinhold Niebuhr responded to these concerns well. Niebuhr was a champion of arguing for the roots of the American Constitution in the doctrine of original sin, though unfortunately his voice has largely been silenced since the 1970s. In a sermon he preached in 1961, he proclaimed: "Finally, there is healthy, but not cynical, realism about our selfishness, Martin Luther said . . . don't be so morbid about the fact that you're selfish; don't deny that you are self-regarding . . . you will be redeemed."[31] This is a freeing word, one that affirms self-worth. No matter how bad I am, I am no more sleazy or selfish, I am no worse, than anyone else. God's love is there for me.

This is also a word that leads to tolerance. My insights about what is good and just are no less free of self-interest than the position of my opponent and debating partner. We need each other to keep each other honest. Later in the sermon Niebuhr put it this way:

> Perhaps we should draw the conclusion that our common life . . . is made tolerable by the knowledge of all this. We are sufferable only when somebody has the power and the courage to stand against us.

> . . . Modern democracy rests upon the insight that what I think to be just is tainted by my own self-interest. I have just enough residual virtue to know that it *is* tainted, and that someone has to stand against me, and declare his different conviction.[32]

Seeing the sin and selfishness that are in me and in my fellow human beings leads me to be a bit more forgiving of, even to get to like, those with whom I am contending.

For Niebuhr, these insights do not undermine radicalism, but entail a critical perspective on government and the prevailing views in society. They inspire an awareness that we must be prophetic critics of all legislation, political proposals, and politically correct social conventions. As he put it in a famous 1941 work: "For without the sinfulness of the human heart in general it is not possible to penetrate through the illusions and pretensions of the successful classes of every age."[33] In other words, without a healthy dose of Augustinian cynicism about human motives, we may be inclined naively to assume that those in power are doing the right thing, even when what they do is exploiting others.

Implicit in these comments, a point Niebuhr makes elsewhere, is the awareness that human beings are so self-preoccupied that it blinds them to the truth about themselves. We are great at fooling ourselves. We actually think that our own agendas and the agendas of society as a whole (if society's agenda is helpful to us personally and to our friends) are not biased. Convinced that we are good, decent, caring human beings who want what is best for everybody, and that our society (insofar as it seems to profit us) is affording equal opportunity to everyone, we are likely to be content with the status quo. It takes the doctrine of original sin to help us recognize that the leaders in society are exercising leadership primarily to help themselves and that the political and ethical commitments we hold dear primarily serve our own self-interests. That can be a wake-up call to examine the foibles, the exploitative tendencies in our own beliefs, perhaps even to recognize how society is exploiting us a lot more than we thought, that we might have more in common with the poor and racial minorities than with the establishment's leaders who we thought were working in our interests. The doctrine of original sin is a mirror to help us know the truth about ourselves and our society.

There is one other contribution that the doctrine of original sin can make in our present social context: an implicit critique of modern America's sense that all that happens is in our own hands, that we freely choose everything that we are, even our loves, passions, and identities. To some extent this point was implicit in Augustine's own reflections on the subject. A major factor in his affirmation of original sin was to make it clear that salvation and love are ultimately out of our hands. The salvation we receive, the good we do, is something that God does to us. Modern Americans, to the extent that we are unconsciously bound to European Enlightenment suppositions and Pelagianism, have a tough time with that affirmation. We think we can make ourselves who we are or what we want to become. We even like to think that love is a choice, that we choose to fall in love and remain in love. But true love, the things we are passionate about, the things that truly define who we are, cannot be so manipulated. A true love, a deep passion, is not something we control.

True love makes lovers do its bidding. Few of us who are truly in love would do all the things we do for our loved ones if love did not compel us. Only people who know that they are in bondage will experience the ecstasy of being compelled to submit happily to the love of their lover in that way, through thick and thin. Only those who know their bondage to sin will find themselves joyful when the love of God or at least the mandate to seek the common good compels them to struggle for justice and serve their communities.

In a paradoxical way, there is something very freeing, even comforting and inspiring, in becoming realistic about human motives, in recognizing that in all that we do, even in all our good deeds, human beings are seeking (sometimes frantically) self-fulfillment. Such an insight helps us become more self-critical, more socially and politically alert, and more tolerant of others' foibles. We are also likely to become more alert to the miracles in life as we marvel that any good can emerge from our sinful, selfish motives.

Augustinian Realism and the American Constitutional System

To make the case for the contribution that the classical Christian, Augustinian view of human nature can make to remedying our present social malaise, we need to assess the philosophical roots of the American constitutional system and the impact of the Augustinian view on it. This analysis also provides insights into why this Augustinian view has largely been silenced in our context. In part this is related to the fact that our constitutional system presupposes an Augustinian view of human persons as concupiscent, which was basic to James Madison's political views, side-by-side with a more optimistic Enlightenment-inspired view of human nature as rational and capable of sound ethical and political action.[1] A starting point for sorting out the interaction of these two depictions of human nature in the American political system needs to be a brief survey of colonial precedents. My aim in this chapter and throughout the book is to argue for more emphasis, especially given our present social realities, on the Augustinian depiction. To the detriment of American society, its uniqueness has largely been blurred in favor of the more Enlightenment-inspired view of human nature.

The Emergence of Competing Strands in the Constitutional System

The first chapter outlined the background of the impact of the Augustinian vision on the American colonies through Puritanism and the philosophy of Scottish Common Sense Realism, advocated especially by John Witherspoon. With Witherspoon's installation as president of the increasingly prestigious College of New Jersey, the previous dominance of the writings of John Locke (1632–1704) and the Idealist philosopher George Berkeley in the curriculum gave way to Common Sense Realism. The influence of Witherspoon and his thought on James Madison when he studied at the college is evident in one of the future founder's 1769 letters, in which he extolled Witherspoon to his father as the one who should come to teach all Madison's fellow Virginians.[2]

Not just on the New Jersey campus did Common Sense Realism exert a significant impact during the colonial era. William Small, an earlier Scottish immigrant to the New World, came to teach at William and Mary College and, as Witherspoon did later, began expounding some of the new Scottish philosophy to his students. One on whom he exerted a great influence was the young Thomas Jefferson.[3]

Other campuses to which the Scottish philosophy and a Presbyterian-Augustinian pessimistic vision of human nature spread were Harvard and the College of Philadelphia in the 1750s (there is evidence that a text by Francis Hutcheson came to be a part of the curriculum of both institutions), as well as, subsequently, to Yale.[4] The philosophical work of Reid's student Dugald Stewart apparently exerted major influence on America's campuses after the Revolution. Testimony to this fact is provided in a letter written by Thomas Jefferson to Stewart in 1824. Jefferson informs him that the Scottish scholar's book had "become the textbook of most of our colleges & academies."[5] It is also interesting to note that as early as 1771 Jefferson was recommending a book by Thomas Reid for a friend's personal library.[6]

The preceding exposition indicates the early impact of John Locke's views on the College of New Jersey. Evidence of his, as well as David Hume's, impact on the founding fathers is abundant. But Locke's impact may not have been as sweeping as many have been led to believe. There seems to be no evidence that his books figured in the set curriculum of any American college before the Revolution.[7] In fact, though Benjamin Franklin recommended a text by Locke on education in his 1749 *Proposals Relating to the Education of Youth in Pennsylvania,* he also recommended texts by Francis Hutcheson pertaining to ethics and government.[8]

Jefferson himself seems to give at least ambiguous praise to Locke's thinking, especially in an 1807 letter to John Norvell. He wrote: "I think there does not exist a good elementary work on the organization of society in civil government. . . . For want of a single work of that character I should recommend Locke on Government."[9]

Despite his only qualified endorsement of Locke's theories of government in this instance, in another letter Jefferson identified Locke as one of the "three greatest men that have ever lived," along with Francis Bacon and Isaac Newton.[10] Some interpreters have argued that this effusive praise of Locke may relate only to Jefferson's appreciation of Locke's work in epistemology and science.[11]

Though the degree to which Jefferson embraced Locke's political theory is in dispute, it is evident that the great British philosopher had a significant impact on the constitutional system, at least on the American Revolution itself and its commitment to compacts or covenants as the basis of government. It is well at this point briefly to review Locke's key commitments in contrast to the Augustinian view.

Trained as a physician, Locke was very much a man of the new (in his era) empirical scientific ethos. He rejected the concept of innate ideas, insisting that "all Ideas come from Sensation or Reflection." The source of all knowledge is empirical, in his view, and we are but "White [blank] papers" furnished with experience.[12] This optimism about the quality of the truth that experience can provide manifested itself in an optimism about what human nature could accomplish, which Locke worked out in his "rational" identification of Christianity with morality.[13] For Locke, all have the ability to save themselves by following the spark of reason in them and the natural law. Everyone has the natural ability to know what is good and to do it. This was a clear break with the Augustinian view of human nature. In fact, Locke's worldview does not really make a place for distinct Christian teachings.[14] The impact of this worldview on American society has been and continues to be of incalculable significance.

With reference to explicit political proposals and observations, Locke offered a number of profound and influential suggestions. Among the most important of these are his insistence that all legitimate government is founded on some sort of "social contract," that its primary aim is to defend property, and that great abuse by governors may justify revolution. In addition, Locke affirmed three distinct powers of government and insisted that we have certain natural rights, including life, liberty, and estate (or property).[15]

A number of influential pamphlets of the Revolution appealed directly to Locke on natural rights, and the preamble to the Constitution seems to presuppose his idea of a social contract as the basis of government.[16] It is evident that there has been some truth to the earlier scholarly consensus regarding Locke's influence on the founders and the system of government they created.

Two other influences on the founders, both relevant for identifying the Augustinianism of the American system, are the Scottish Enlightenment philosopher David Hume (1711–1776) and the French political philosopher Baron de Montesquieu (Charles-Louis de Secondat; 1689–1755). Both had an Augustinian-like pessimism about human nature. Hume's was a skeptical reaction against Locke's optimism, both with regard to epistemology (he did not believe that we can attain absolute and certain truth through our experience) and with regard to human nature and governmental theory. About the latter range of issues, he wrote:

> In contriving any system of government, and fixing the several checks and controls of the constitution, every man ought to be supposed a *knave,* and to have no other end, in all his actions, than private interest. By this interest we must govern him, and by means of it, make him, notwithstanding his insatiable avarice and ambition, cooperate to public good.[17]

The stress here on private interest and insatiable avarice is certainly most suggestive of the Presbyterian heritage in which Hume was nurtured and of Augustinian thinking about the concupiscent nature of human beings and actions. There are echoes of the constitutional separation of powers here.

Montesquieu made similar Augustinian points. Much like the African Father, he warned that power corrupts. He maintained that to provide a good balance, three branches of government are desirable.[18]

There are a number of occasions when several of the founders refer to the thought of these men. Benjamin Franklin had a regular pattern of correspondence with Hume as the two became acquainted while serving in diplomatic service for their nations in France. In one letter, Franklin praises Hume's essay on the jealousy of commerce, referring to how it may promote "selfish Man" (note the Augustinianism in this phrase) to seek the common good.[19]

In his own correspondence, Jefferson expressed general, though qualified, regard for Hume's work on the history of the English people and for Montesquieu's work.[20] Jefferson especially criticized the latter for seeming to opt for a plural executive branch, rather than for a single chief executive officer as the U.S. Constitution finally created.[21] James Madison's appropriation of the great French thinker's work was also evident at a crucial point, as he cited Montesquieu in support of his argument in favor of the separation of powers in the three branches of the federal government.[22]

Not surprisingly, given the impressive intellect of the most prominent leaders, the American founders were influenced by a rich diversity. Consequently, both of the competing strands of thought that have been identified pertaining to human nature and governmental theory are evident in the American political system.

The American System's Appropriation of the Competing Strands of Thought

A survey of America's founding documents reveals the presence of the competing strands of thought we have identified. An Enlightenment-oriented, optimistic portrayal of what human beings can accomplish, of how they can establish their own government and know what is good and just, coupled with a preoccupation with individual human rights, is foundational to the American system. But side by side with this strand is a set of assumptions more compatible with Christianity and the Augustinian view of human nature as essentially selfish and so requiring a government to check human concupiscence for the sake of the common good.

The Enlightenment's optimistic view of human nature seems embedded in both the Bill of Rights and the Declaration of Independence. In both documents we find echoes of Locke's concern with human rights. Consider the Declaration's reference to "certain unalienable Rights." (The British philosopher's enumeration of the natural rights of "life, liberty, and estate" were amended slightly in the Declaration to "Life, Liberty, and the Pursuit of Happiness.") Also reflected in the Declaration is Locke's insistence that the only legitimate basis for government is a contract with the people. The Declaration implies this with its reference to the "consent of the governed."

Several significant references to this optimistic view of humanity are evident in some of the founders' writings relevant to the political system they created. A 1783 circular letter by George Washington reflects this optimism and a fervent belief typical of the view that we can freely determine our own fate. He wrote:

> The citizens of America . . . are, from this period, to be considered as the actors on a most conspicuous theatre, which seems to be peculiarly designated by providence for the display of greatness and felicity. . . . The foundation of our empire was not laid in the gloomy age of ignorance and superstition, but at an epoch when the rights of mankind were better understood and more clearly defined, than at any former period. . . . At this auspicious period, the United States came into existence as a nation, and if their citizens should not be completely free and happy, the fault will be entirely their own.

In *The Federalist Papers* (No. 3) one finds instances of this Enlightenment optimism. John Jay referred to Americans as "intelligent and well-informed" and said that such people are unlikely to hold erroneous opinions about their own self-interest for a long period of time.

In his endorsement of this sort of optimism, Thomas Jefferson went to the extreme of believing in the possibility of the unchecked progress of human beings. In a 1799 letter, he wrote:

> I consider man as formed for society, and endowed by nature with those dispositions which fit him for society. I believe also with Condorcet, as mentioned in your letter, that his mind is perfectible to a degree of which we cannot as yet form any conception.

> I join you therefore in branding as cowardly the idea that the human mind is incapable of further advances. . . .

> For as long as we may think as we will and speak as we think, the condition of man will proceed in improvement.[23]

The founders thought that their own generation was virtuous. But at least they were realistic about subsequent generations, and in fact they sought to establish a government predicated on the attempt to protect the American people from less virtuous leaders who would follow.[24]

The perceived need to deal with less virtuous leaders is a function of the founders' endorsement of an Augustinian view of human nature. About this matter, James Bryce wrote:

> Someone has said that the American government and constitution are based on the theology of Calvin and the philosophy of Thomas Hobbes. This at least is true, that there is a hearty Puritanism in the view of human nature which pervades the instrument of 1787. It is the work of men who believed in original sin. . . .[25]

Examples of America's founders maintaining Augustinian convictions, especially as prefigured by Witherspoon (see introduction) are abundant. Among those offering remarks that presupposed an Augustinian-like vision of human nature were Madison, Gouverneur Morris (who warned against the rich seeking to establish dominion over everyone else), Alexander Hamilton (who claimed that "men love power"), and Benjamin Franklin (who reminded delegates that men are driven by "ambition and avarice").[26] Franklin made a similar point in interpreting virtues in an Augustinian sense, as a kind of expression of concupiscence. He wrote: "Almost every Man has a strong Desire of being valu'd and esteem'd by the rest of his Species."[27]

In two of his contributions to *The Federalist Papers*, Madison generalized these Augustinian observations, applying them to groups (factions) that emerge in any free society.[28] Madison's *Preface to Debates in the Convention* refers to "the weakness and wants of man naturally leading to an association of individuals" and to "feeble communities" resorting to a Union.[29]

It is true that Madison also extolled the human capacity for virtue alongside depravity as necessary for self-government. Some have appealed to this passage as an indication that he broke with the views of his Presbyterian teacher in favor Enlightenment optimism.[30] However, he simply embodies the general endorsement of the founders in toto of both the Christian and the Enlightenment strands of thought. Indeed, even historic Christianity has not ruled out the reality of human goodness in the midst of sin (Gen. 1:31).

Another way in which we find an Augustinian vision of human nature in Madison's thought is in his appreciation of the herd mentality of the public. This was a crucial supposition for his contention that we need government structures to protect us from the tyranny of the mob:

> If it be true that all governments rest on opinion, it is no less true that the strength of opinion in each individual, and its practical influence on his conduct, depend much on the number which he supposes to have entertained the same opinion. The reason of man, like man himself, is timid and cautious when left alone, and acquires firmness and confidence in proportion to the number with which it is associated.[31]

This same caution regarding the need to share power, lest corruption emerge or some segment of the population (especially the majority) assume an undue balance of power and transgress the rights of minorities, underlies the collective thinking of the American founders. A few further words of caution by Madison on the tyranny of the majority are in order:

> Different interests necessarily exist in different classes of citizens. If a majority be united by a common interest, the rights of the minority will be insecure.[32]

> ... there are particular moments in public affairs when the people, stimulated by some irregular passion, or some illicit advantage, or misled by the artful representations of interested men, may call for measures which they themselves will afterwards be the most ready to lament and condemn.[33]

Alexander Hamilton likewise fretted about how the majority was prone to give "unqualified complaisance to every sudden breeze of passion, or to every transient impulse which the people may receive from the arts of men, who flatter their prejudices to betray their interests."[34] The Augustinian character of these reflections is quite apparent.

There is another way in which the American political system reflects commitments compatible with Augustine's political philosophy. Because self-interest is the name of the game in government in both Augustine's and the founders' views, it follows that the state is not a realm in which love can be legislated. For love is spontaneous, but obedience to the natural law that mandates concern with the common good must be compelled. (The "self-evident truths" of the Declaration of Independence bespeak a basis of natural law for our governmental system. Appeals to common sense and the natural law are also made at several crucial points in *The Federalist Papers*.)[35]

In connection with government's role in compelling this sort of obedience, a basic principle of the American constitutional system is that we need to separate the powers in order to coerce compromises that can make possible the achievement of the common good (what the Constitution calls the "general Welfare"). If we do not, the most powerful factions in the nation, because they are self-interested and concupiscent, will have their own way in American laws to the detriment of weaker segments of the population. We see this commitment most clearly articulated in one of Madison's contributions to *The Federalist Papers*. He wrote:

> Justice is the end of government. It is the end of civil society. . . .
> In the extended republic of the United States, and among the great variety of interests, parties, and sects which it embraces, a coalition of the majority of the whole society could seldom take place on any other principles than those of justice and the general good; whilst there being thus less danger to a minor from the will of the major party, there must be less pretext, also, to provide for the security of the former, by introducing into the government a will not dependent on the latter, or, in other words, a will independent of the society itself.[36]

If the branches of government are separate, each with its own self-interest in maintaining power and influence, the founders hypothesized, then it would be harder for the self-ish interests of each to reach agreements that would be beneficial to just one segment of the population. The coalitions necessary to create national policies would have to take into account the interests of a broader spectrum of society, and so would more nearly lead to just decisions. Note Madison's realism. He does not claim that the system will always work that way. He simply contends that it will be harder for a self-interested group to get its way at the expense of society as a whole.

Basic to these reflections is Madison's and the other founders' belief in the need to be watchful of self-interested segments of the population, because all people are selfish (self-interested, concupiscent). Just as obvious is their commitment to prioritizing the common good over private interests, a commitment to justice in line with the law of God, which the founders believed is rooted in nature and reason. In this regard, they affirmed another of Augustine's commitments.[37]

Another instance in which the Augustinian strand seems evident in the constitutional system is the founders' break with Locke's insistence that the only proper basis for legitimate government is a social contract among the citizens. They embraced instead the Scottish Common Sense Realist notion (which, recall, reflects the Calvinist perspective) that if a government functions efficiently and legally, it does so only because a kind of contract between the people and the rulers has been assumed—a kind of "tacit consent" of the governed.[38] We see this viewpoint expressed by Madison at the Constitutional Convention. In one of his speeches, he claimed:

> A law violating a constitution established by the people themselves, would be considered by the Judges as null and void. . . . The doctrine laid down by the law of Nations in the case of treaties is that a breach of one article by any of the parties, frees the other parties from their engagements. In the case of a union of people under one Constitution, the nature of one pact has always been understood to exclude such an interpretation.[39]

In fact, Madison argued the case for the perpetuity of the Constitution. In making this point we see that for all the similarities between the concept of tacit consent and a contractual theory of government, one important difference in emphasis is at stake. The concept of social contract can be taken as requiring annual or regular renewal by the people. Not so with Madison's concept of tacit consent. In a 1790 letter to Jefferson, in response to his colleague's advocacy of revising constitutions for each generation, Madison even invoked Reid's concept of "tacit consent":

> May it not be questioned whether it be possible to exclude wholly the idea of tacit consent, without subverting the foundation of civil Society?—on what principle does the voice of the majority bind the minority? It does not result I conceive from the Law of nature, but from compact founded on conveniency. . . . If this assent cannot be given tacitly, or be not implied where no positive evidence forbids, persons born in Society would not on attaining ripe age be bound by acts of the Majority, and either a *unanimous* repetition of every law would be necessary on the occasion of new members, or an express assent must be obtained from these to the rule by which the voice of the Majority is made the voice of the whole.[40]

Think of it. This is the way in which the Constitution has functioned in the American system throughout the republic's history. No law can be passed that contradicts it or negates it. The Constitution need not be ratified anew each year. In that sense, anyone who lives in America and is governed by its laws gives "tacit consent" to the Constitution and the founders' decision about it.

The perpetuity of the Constitution was essentially mandated by the founders' Augustinian vision of human nature, which entails a suspicion of the will of the majority and its tendency to be moved by "every sudden breeze of passion," particularly those that flatter the majority's interests. They had a point, did they not? Consider how quickly American public opinion can flit, from concern about ecology (during the last gas shortage) to demand for bigger cars and higher speed limits on the interstate highways, from the 1960s passion for justice to today's pro-business ethos, from rhetoric about the quality of life to today's always-on-the-job (24/7) ethos. The only way to keep things from getting out of hand, lest the next American passion be for the indentured servanthood of immigrants or for a more "efficient," less open news media, is to maintain the Constitution and its Bill of Rights as a check against such passions.

Concupiscence leads individuals to do dumb things sometimes, because what we want is not always synonymous with what is best for us. (The Christian doctrine of sin, particularly St. Paul's lament in Romans 7:19 that he does not do the good he wants, but instead does the evil he does not want, makes this point clear.) Consequently, the American system was structured to take this into account, and so the system compels Americans to do some things that the majority at any given time may not desire. The Augustinian Christian view of human nature stands in the background of many things the government makes us do (pay taxes, set suspects free on legal technicalities, give preference to minorities).

A further point at which the Augustinian strand seems more influential on the American system than does the Lockean-Enlightenment vision is evident in the founders' break with the British philosopher's correlation of civil liberties with the ownership of property. Certainly some of the founders, even Madison, were open to property qualifications for voters and insisted that government is instituted to protect property as much as to protect individuals.[41] Even these commitments, though, are clearly subordinated in the Constitution to the concern for the common good, insofar as property qualifications for voting are not reflected in the document, and its preamble asserts that the American government has been created to serve the common good for "ourselves and *our posterity*" [italics added]. In this respect, the Constitution reflects the position of the Presbyterian (and so Augustinian-influenced) Scottish Common Sense Realism. Its chief spokesman, Thomas Reid, in clear distinction from Locke, wrote that "private Property ought to yield to Publick Good where there is repugnancy between them."[42]

Benjamin Franklin also subordinated private property to the common good. This is evident in his 1783 letter to Robert Morris. He wrote:

> All property, indeed, except the Savage's temporary Cabin, his Bow, his Matchcoat, . . . seems to me to be Creature of public Convention. Hence the Public has the Right of Regulating Descents, and all other Conveyances of Property, and even of limiting the Quantity and Uses of it. All the Property that is necessary to a Man, for the Conservation of the Individual and the Propagation of the Species, is his natural Right which none can justly deprive him of: But all Property superfluous to such purposes is the Property of the Publick, who may therefore by other Laws dispose of it, whenever the Welfare of the Publick shall demand such Disposition.[43]

Likewise, Jefferson—at least in a 1785 letter to James Madison—even advocated the redistribution of property:

> I am conscious that an equal division of property is impracticable, but the consequences of this enormous inequality producing so much misery to the bulk of mankind, legislators cannot invent too many devices for subdividing property, only taking care to let their subdivisions go hand in hand with natural affections of the human mind. . . . Whenever there are in any country uncultivated lands and unemployed poor, it is clear that the laws of property have been so far extended as to violate natural right. . . . If for the encouragement of industry we allow it [the land] to be appropriated, we must take care that other employment be provided to those excluded from the appropriation.[44]

A concern that the poor be protected in property transactions has ancient roots in the Christian tradition and so was affirmed also by Thomas Reid and Common Sense Realism.[45] Even Locke had similar commitments, to the point of proposing that whatever extra property cannot be used by its owner should "belong to others."[46]

It seems evident that America's founders were not advocates of a laissez-faire economics like Adam Smith's, but actually saw a role for the state in shaping economic policy (not unlike Keynesian economics), even going so far as to advocate redistributing wealth to the poor.[47] This raises the question of why there has been and is notably at present a sentiment against government engagement in shaping economic policy on behalf of the poor. It has to do with the "secularist" way in which the Enlightenment strand and its optimistic individualism indebted to Locke, along with his concern with the links between government and property, have been appropriated. The optimism associated with Locke's view of human nature makes it easy to conclude that we can make our own way in the world without help and, consequently, that those at society's bottom deserve to be there. Only these dimensions of Locke's thought are invoked in our present context, while his profound sense that property is properly used only when it is administered in accord with the divine law is conveniently overlooked. As a result, the two distinct visions of human nature that are part of the American constitutional heritage have largely manifested in two distinct views of government's role in regulating commerce and other rights.

We have already noted the impact of the Lockean-Enlightenment preoccupation with human rights on the Bill of Rights. It is also important to note how in the first amendments, limited government is advocated. The Tenth Amendment ensures that the federal government not arrogate for itself any powers not expressly delegated to it or prohibited to the states by the Constitution. Those powers not mentioned were to be the province of local (state) governments. In addition, references in the Constitution to the federal government's role in regulating the economy and the privileges of the states (Art. I, Secs. 8, 9, 10), the separation of powers, and the binding character of the Constitution (the concept of tacit consent), bespeak the Augustinian and federalist strand of the Constitution.[48]

The Federalist Papers testify to an awareness of the presence of the two strands in the Constitution. Madison referred to both the federal and national character of the new government. The former would provide stability in the new American system. Its national character, a sense of an American people, would provide the new system with energy. The Constitution itself, the new government's federal character, would provide stability because it was to be established in perpetuity. In Paper #37, Madison made the point about these two strands in the Constitution even more concisely. He wrote:

> Among the difficulties encountered by the [Constitutional] convention, a very important one must have lain, in combining the requisite stability and energy in government with the inviolable attention due to liberty and to the republican form. . . . Energy in government is essential to that security against external and internal danger, and to that prompt and salutary execution of the laws which enter into the very definition of good government. Stability in government, is essential to national character, and to the advantages annexed to it, as well as to that repose and confidence in the minds of the people, which are among the chief blessings of civil society.[49]

What Has Become of the Two Strands?

In a sense, the analysis of our present situation in the introduction has answered the question posed in this section's title. Because the two strands in the American political system are in conflict, the history of American society might be interpreted as their ongoing competition for dominance. Insofar as the more Enlightenment-based strand tends to favor smaller government, while the more Christian-based Augustinian strand implies the need for stronger federal controls of an otherwise unruly, concupiscent mob, their ongoing competition throughout American history is evident.

The Augustine in me believes that it may be the genius of our system that these two strands have been affirmed and encouraged to check and balance each other. The problem with our present era, then, is that the social currents in the air—the therapeutic and narcissistic dynamics—have so discredited and effectively silenced the Christian-Augustinian side of the American system that the more Enlightenment-based secular-democratic consciousness has become, in practice, the only real American option.

There is a great deal at stake in the silencing of the Christian-Augustinian nature of the Constitution. Without that strand, the American system and our society will begin to confer all authority on the will of the people, on the majority, with full confidence in their wisdom. As government shrinks as a result, there will be fewer and fewer checks and balances of the current majority's will. As Madison has taught us, when that happens, because of the self-interested character of human beings, the majority will begin to act tyrannically at the expense of the minority. When we consider the extent to which the pro-business majority is exercising that sort of influence in America today at the expense of the working poor and the squeezed middle class, we may already be encountering this constitutional crisis.

Some manifestations of the deleterious social impact of the discrediting of the Christian-Augustinian strand have already been noted. The rest of this book provides more details to this initial intuition and proceeds to show how recovering the Augustinian strand of thought can help America deal with its current social ills.

three

Politics with Glitz, but without Much Constitutional Common Sense

In significant ways, political discourse and prevailing models of political participation have been conducted without an appreciation of the American constitutional system's realism. I contend that this is in large part a factor in the widespread American distrust and neglect of our political system. The present ethos also values small government, permits special interests (especially big business and wealth) to exert disproportionate influence, and elects candidates with media charisma (those with a celebrity quality about them).

The emergence of these trends is related to the capitulation of the public to the German Enlightenment suppositions regarding the fundamental goodness of human nature and the priority of the individual's immediate gratification and rights over the common good. When present political dynamics fail to witness to fundamental human goodness or achieve complete fulfillment for us, when we do not get all that we want from government, we become cynical. But this is a negative, nihilistic cynicism. It is not the realistic cynicism of Augustine and the Constitution, which stimulates us to get into the trenches to seek justice. This is clearly the present political frame of mind of most Americans.

69

Ain't Nobody Who Trusts the Government Anymore

It is not the best of times to be to involved in politics. A January 1997 Gallup poll revealed that those in Congress had high or very high trust among only 14 percent of the American public, the very lowest of all occupations, even lower than business executives and lawyers. (Pharmacists were the big winner as the most trusted occupational group, gaining 64 percent of the public trust.) This is a phenomenal drop from 1986 and 1977, when Congress had been as high as the 40th percentile.[1] A more recent (January 1999) Gallup poll provided a no less gloomy picture. It indicated that only 7 percent of the American public had a great deal of confidence in those in political life, and nearly one-third of the public had very little confidence. (The figures were only slightly higher the next year, as a mere 11 percent of the public expressed a great deal of trust in the Congress.)[2] Certainly this distrust of government is reflected in ever lower levels of voter turnout, seen most dramatically in a dip in voter participation in presidential elections from the high of 70 percent of voters in the nineteenth century to the low of barely above 50 percent in the 1990s and in the 2000 election.

Of course, if we are persuaded that people are basically good and that the will of the majority (which we in turn consider the most reliable authority, because good people should always be self-determining), then we will inevitably be disappointed with all the wheeling-dealing and compromises involved in politics. On the other hand, an Augustinian view of human nature is realistically cynical enough to appreciate that politics is ultimately about power and that you get things done by means of tradeoffs and coalitions in which you engage to get power.

This loss of confidence in political leaders is reflected in the polls' indication of the public's general loss of respect for those in the classical professions. For reasons indicated below, some of this is deserved. But in a culture in which everyone yearns for the celebrity that the media seem to suggest we can all attain, it is harder for narcissist celebrity-seekers to admire power and charisma in others.

Of course, the tragic events of September 11, 2001, with its terrorism and the federal government's generally commendable response, coupled with President Bush's politically astute strategies for rallying American public opinion to his campaign against terrorism, markedly enhanced the government's standing in opinion polls. A *Washington Post* poll conducted soon after the tragedy revealed a thirty-five-year high of 64 percent of Americans expressing belief that the federal government does the right thing "nearly always" or "most of the time." This development neither heralds a new day in general cynicism toward government nor is surprising from an Augustinian vantage point. We have already noted that James Madison believed that concupiscent people like us are readily swayed by the latest passion and interest.[3] Certainly a lot of passions were stirred and directed by American leaders during the months following the terrorist episodes. But it is doubtful that such confidence will be sustained, just as the elder Bush's high popularity was not sustained after its Gulf War surge. An April 2002 Gallup poll registering a 30 percent decline in the public's confidence in Congress since a month after the September 11 terrorism (from 84 percent to 57 percent approval) suggests that the popularity of the federal government in general after the September 11, 2001, invasions is not to be sustained.[4]

The government's new popularity cannot be totally divorced from the help it gave the businesses affected by the airline crashes or the generous bailouts it provided the ailing airline industry. Thus, this surge in popularity during the early stages of the younger Bush's administration may indicate how thoroughly controlled American public opinion is by big business.

In any event, the most recent surge in confidence in government is still just a blip on the screen when one examines the long-term picture of negative public attitudes toward government since the mid-1980s. Yet even during years when it was most cynical about government, the American public has been a lot kinder to itself when it comes to its trust in the electorate for making choices on election day. According to an April 2000 survey conducted by Yankelovich Partners, Inc., for American University, less than a third had only little trust in the electorate's choices. Sixty-six percent had at least a fair amount of trust. In the same poll only 32 percent deemed today's candidates excellent or good, 48 percent deemed them average, and 17 percent viewed them as poor or very poor.[5] Americans, like everybody else, are better at seeing the waywardness of others (their politicians) than at seeing it in themselves (the voters). Of course, the Christian doctrine of sin would have us expect exactly that (Matt. 7:3–5).

Celebrity Politics

Politicians and government may have lost a lot of public respect, but there are still plenty of office seekers, especially for federal and state offices. Why, if it's such an unappreciated job?

Politics, like the professions, has always drawn people with mixed motives. Of course there is the "pure" motive of wanting to help people. But the concupiscent desire for power and influence, for prestige and respect, cannot be denied as a motive for seeking public office or a professional position. And since the dawn of the television age, perhaps most notably since the Kennedy presidency, the concupiscent desires have taken a new turn. Politicians, like some other members of the social elite, have become celebrities, and politics has become filled with glitz (and lacking in content).

In a 1977 book the eminent sociologist Richard Sennett described how a kind of privatism has emerged in American society that challenges social conventions of decency.[6] These dynamics help us to understand further how far-reaching the therapeutic and narcissist models of being are in America today, and how they have even permeated our politics.

In essence, Sennett's thesis is that early modern Western culture was characterized by certain social conventions of politeness and formality, which by today's therapeutic canons are regarded as constricting and artificial. These conventions allowed people of distinct backgrounds and social classes to strike up conversations and to cooperate in common projects while maintaining their innermost secrets. Besides, it was believed, people of character share many common traits. Beginning in the nineteenth century, with the rise of the philosophy of romanticism, which taught the elite that the essence of their humanity was in their feelings and that everyone has a unique personality, these conventions began to break down. (The core suppositions of romanticism assume a positive, optimistic assessment of human nature and its capacities.)[7]

By no means did the conventions of Victorian society and American Puritanism wither away immediately, as they remained largely in place through much of the twentieth century. However, romanticism gradually made an impact on American society, not least of all in the development of romantic love and public expressions of affection. Its other manifestations are evident in the new forms of anxiety that accompany an awareness that one ought to be unique and that the expression of one's feelings needs to be guarded, as they uniquely reveal who one is.

As a result, great interest began to be taken in the biographies, and even the image, of some of our political leaders. Yet there were still some things that a person did not say in public and certainly did not expect politicians or other leaders (like pastors or doctors) to reveal either. There was a mystique about leaders, about everyone Americans encountered (including and particularly those of the opposite sex). We are more "familiar" with each other today. What happened, and does it really enhance community and our democratic system?

With the end of World War II and the popularization of Freud, as well as the mass distribution of television, the seeds of romanticism already planted in America became viable enough to supplant the old conventions. In their place, the therapeutic ethos demanded a cult of authenticity. It has effectively torn away for many the (benign) masks everyone used to wear in public. Much conversation now takes the form of confession (it's "touchy-feely"). Consequently, our jobs and our personal interactions become primarily conceived of as vehicles for self-realization, just as the narcissist uses people and the tasks of life to that end.

Today's politicians, Sennett claimed, are obligated to follow these mores, to reveal their inner lives in public. Bill Clinton was certainly a master of this. Jimmy Carter's personal confession of lust illustrates these trends too. John Kennedy endeared himself to the American public not so much because of what he did, but because of his biography (as war hero) and his family (as we fell in love with Jackie and the Kennedy children). Of course, as Kennedy and Clinton proved, we do not know the celebrity as well as we think. Actually, there is a sense in which we got to know people better under the old conventions than we do today, because the old conventions made substantive discussions of issues possible. Disagreements are more socially tolerable when politeness in interactions is mandated and when there is a certain distance between one's personhood and one's ideas. If political disagreements can be conducted politely, if differences over policies are not challenges to the opponent's personhood, then such differences are dealt with in a well-mannered way that today's therapeutic climate does not readily tolerate.

With these developments, Sennett argued, politics is no longer primarily about ideas and what you get done. It is more about manipulating images and developing an admiring group of supporters. This is narcissism in the political realm.

As I have already suggested, the tendency to regard politicians as celebrities is simply a manifestation of broader cultural trends. In a way, we can say that we became asphyxiated with celebrities with the advent of TV. To be sure there were movie stars and sports stars (political stars too) before the days of TV. But there was a certain mystery about them. With television they have come into our living rooms. We are given the illusion of knowing them personally. We see them every day.[8] We admire them; we want to be like them; we crave the excitement of their lives. Yet in reality we do not know them at all.

Given the admiration American society has developed for entertainment and sports celebrities, it is hardly surprising that in the television age, politicians realized the need to (or else they yearned to) become celebrities. Granted, the radio made Franklin D. Roosevelt a celebrity to some extent (as we came to think we knew his family life, which of course we did not in full). John Kennedy, though, with his good looks and youthful effervescence, was the first true celebrity president. Since his administration, every successor and prominent politician has needed to become a celebrity. Those who could star in the media and manipulate it have become the best politicians. Witness the popularity of Reagan and Clinton, the demise of Gingrich, and the failure of Gore. Consider also the political careers of stars like Clint Eastwood and Sonny Bono.

Celebrities need to change images, adjust. Such a culture has no loyalty. For celebrities, who you seem to be is more important than what you say or believe. Ratings count more than substance. This is a familiar scenario for today's politicians, who need an image to gain popularity and need to continue to cultivate that image. That image must be in line with the fashions of the media elite. Consider how the image that Jimmy Carter projected on his way to the White House fit the post-Nixon era, but his "Mr. Clean, Committed Christian" was not attractive to most media elite. It played as weakness. Since leaving office he has framed a new image, "The Greatest Ex-President." That plays. The public and the media love him again. Yet when one considers his significant accomplishments in international affairs as president (such as the Camp David Accord), has he really been that much more successful since 1980? His new *image* plays better.

How about the great media manipulator Ronald Reagan? He remains popular; his image lives beyond the new realities of his current fragile condition. The people loved Reagan. What has been called "voodoo economics" led to the recession that Bush the elder inherited, but his image was far more important than his policies.

Much American foreign policy since World War II has been about images and perceptions that Americans and their rivals wanted to project and maintain. The Vietnam War was fought not to win, but to preserve America's image. Clinton's foreign interventions were not clearly in America's interests, but they did aim to maintain the image of America as the world's sole superpower.

Just as most celebrities (such as Top 40 performers) have their day and pass away, so our politicians are also a passing fancy. The decreasing significance of and loyalty to political parties makes perfect sense in our narcissistic culture of celebrity. These dynamics also explain how quickly we tire of our politicians and become cynical about them. Maybe they deserve it. Perhaps Americans have always been suspicious of those who govern. But if ideas were more important than the image of the messengers of those ideas, would American public opinion be quite so fickle?

The idea of politicians as celebrities has led some prominent political leaders to act like stereotypical Hollywood celebrities in their personal lifestyles. Lest we make Bill Clinton too much the whipping-boy, consider former Representative Gary Condit of California or Georgia's Bob Barr (that self-proclaimed paragon of political virtue, now on wife number three). The remarks made during these scandals by commentators in the know that affairs by members of Congress are hardly new speak volumes about the impact of narcissism on American life. Even an insider like Representative Christopher Shays of Connecticut confirmed these observations when he claimed in a July 15, 2001, broadcast of CNN's *Late Edition* that if "infidelity is the test, there would be a number of members of Congress that should resign." We have come a long way from 1960, when Nelson Rockefeller could not gain the Republican nomination for president because he had divorced and remarried (without a hint of scandal).

One of the outcomes of these dynamics is that Americans in the celebrity culture tend to elect the rich and famous. Sometimes those celebrities represent the interests of the majority of voters. But does it not seem strange that the class interests of particular voters count no more than the star quality of the candidates? That is not the way the American founders thought the system would work. If Americans feel estranged from their government, and if it does not seem to be representing the public's interests, then perhaps that is because we elect our favorite celebrities and not those who best represent our interests.

It is evident how celebrity-oriented our politics have become. At least two implications follow from this. First, it further contributes to America's lack of respect for government and its leaders. We may be in awe of celebrities, but we do not always respect them. We know our politicians' and the political processes' weaknesses better now than we did in the pre-television, pre-computer age. No wonder we do not respect our leaders as much as did the constituents of Washington, Lincoln, John Adams, and even Woodrow Wilson. That public did not know their leaders' weaknesses, their humanity.

The other implication of the celebrity character of present American politics is really a core presupposition of these dynamics. The idea of celebrity, the veneration of one whom we yearn to be like, presupposes a veneration of human goodness or at least a positive assessment of human nature. Celebrities are a little like us. We know them so well that we (at least secretly) aspire to be like them. Besides, the media provide us with opportunities to experience their fame and glory, sparking in us the craving for such titillating experience. In principle, we can be as good—or at least as glamorous—as they are. After all, in a reflected sense the media allow us to experience what they have. Consequently, in loving our celebrities we are loving ourselves (our human potential). And we do love our celebrities—at least for awhile.

Celebrity politics also contributes to the fickleness of American public opinion. Just as we flit from one celebrity to another, we are likely to flit from one political interest to another (or to none at all). By contrast, an Augustinian appreciation of human selfishness would move us away from concentrating so much on the personality of the messenger of our political commitments and toward the message, the political issues themselves. When we are a little cynical about human nature, we do not get so hung up on celebrities. We realize that political issues are bigger than the flaws of their proponents. It is hard to do that in a therapeutically oriented context, one as focused on personality as modern America is.

The celebrity culture, the cult of personality, makes elections all the more important, indeed perhaps the most important part of politics. The very nature of the media intensifies the importance of elections. For the media, as we shall note, crave the sensational, which is often trivial, at the expense of the substantive. The horse race of the election is a lot more exciting; it plays on the tube and in the papers much better than the issues that are debated. As a result, given the media's dominance as America's chief opinion maker, it is little wonder that so much attention is given to the polls during election time, and so little to the issues. There are other dynamics in our present election processes that have caused much cynicism and that in turn explain some of the present priorities of the federal government. Again, an Augustinian view of human nature helps us better understand these dynamics.

The Degradation of the Electoral Process: Image and Business

Political consultants, insiders in the process, believe that part of the problem with our politics today pertains to the public. A June 1999 survey conducted by Yankelovich Partners, Inc., for American University revealed that only 3 percent of consultants deemed the public to be well informed; 61 percent were convinced that it is somewhat poorly or very poorly informed. Of course, 79 percent of them still trusted the public's judgment in elections.[9] This may be a reflection of consultants' (adulterated) optimism about human nature. Or it could reflect the consultants' Augustinian realism: that despite the obvious failings of the public, the system still basically works. Still, polls indicate that the public is becoming less interested in and less informed about politics (having slumped by one-fifth in political interest from 1975 to 1999, with post–baby boom generations a third less likely than their elders to be politically informed).[10]

The cult of celebrity is further strengthened by the sense that the American public is not informed and so is not interested in debating the crucial issues of the day. Such reticence to engage in this sort of political discourse fits the general tenor of our day, which prefers superficial or apparent compromise and cooperation to the hammering out of just and genuine compromises and policies.

Of course, shying away from debate in favor of surface-level compromise and cooperation relates to current business-management techniques (which, as we shall see, stress "teamwork") and to our therapeutic ethos, which stresses positive feelings and affirmation, not confrontation. Somehow a debate between conflicting factions is perceived as bad manners. In addition, the media—the primary means of political communication in our context—do not lend themselves to dialogue about complex issues. Sound bites work better. This further feeds the cult of political celebrity. When issues are not the focus of political action, attention turns to the players, and the one who is the most charismatic or charming, who has the best media personality, gets the most attention.

All of these dynamics—a sense that only national celebrities have real influence on government, that the issues do not really count or are too complex for the general public to understand—have had an impact on the level of the public's engagement in the political process. The narcissism of our therapeutic era plays a role. As a result, or perhaps because these dynamics have emerged in consequence of the public's retreat from local civic engagement, from 1970 to 1995 there was a decrease in participation in community activities pertaining to local political campaigns, service clubs, and school affairs.[11]

Both the consultants and the public see that part of the problem with the electoral process is broadcast journalism, as 52 percent of those surveyed rated broadcast journalists as poor or very poor (17 percent regarding them as good to excellent). The print journalists ranked much higher, not much below national party organizations. Fifty-five percent considered the way that the news media reports on politics the main factor in voter cynicism, outweighing the poor performance of today's politicians (39 percent), negative campaigning (39 percent), and fund-raising (34 percent).[12]

The public was a bit kinder, as only 20 percent deemed such broadcast journalists as poor or very poor, and 37 percent deemed them good.[13] Both these consultants and the public believed that there is too much unethical campaigning; 70 percent thought it happens at least fairly often; and 91 percent, at least sometimes.[14] A survey of political consultants revealed that 73 percent thought that unethical practices happen sometimes in political consulting, while 24 percent believed they happen at least fairly often.[15]

Dirty politics and negative campaigning have always been with us, contrary to contemporary American perceptions. One need not stop with the elder Bush's infamous Willie Horton ad in the 1988 election or with Lyndon Johnson's 1964 TV ad against Barry Goldwater, which visually implied that the Republican would lead Americans to nuclear war. One can go back to the nineteenth century, to the 1884 presidential election, in which Republicans attacked Democrat Grover Cleveland for fathering an illegitimate child. Democrats responded with a rhyme concerning the Republican candidate:

> Blaine, Blaine, James G. Blaine;
> the continental liar from the state of Maine.

Blaine's supporters, most notably a Presbyterian clergyman named Buchard, declared that a vote for Cleveland was a vote for "Rum, Romanism and Rebellion." Nearly a century earlier, during Washington's administration, Congressman John Randolph said about a fellow member of Congress, "He shines and stinks like rotten mackerel by moonlight."[16]

We need to examine why we are convinced that negative campaigning is so much worse today. One factor is the tendency of humans to idealize the past, to see the present as worse than the past. But we must consider, above any other factor, that today's therapeutic ethos and the optimistic view of human beings that goes with it raises expectations so high that we are shocked to find that candidates do what it takes to win. We have become so cynical about government because without the Constitution's Augustinian appreciation of the selfishness of human beings we are shocked by partisanship and by our politicians' quest for power. We would not be so shocked, but would instead be more realistic about politics, if we were more Augustinian.

We should be suspicious about the impact of special interests. This is evident in the growing influence of Political Action Committees (PACs) on the political process. In 1981–1982 PACs contributed only $61.1 million to House candidates and $22.6 million to Senate candidates. By 1997–1998 the figures had swelled to $158.7 million and $48.1 million, respectively—double the earlier amounts.[17]

In this connection the dominance of American business in government needs to be considered. Certainly the growing dominance of economic preoccupations in popular culture (discussed later in more detail) is a factor. It has been facilitated politically by the way in which business's aims and those of the Religious Right (and other culturally conservative constituencies) converge. The Religious Right's focus on conventional morality, family, sex, crime, drugs, and education fits nicely with business. This agenda not only promises to provide businesses with productive, pliant, and reliable workers, but also leaves business pretty much alone, without having to worry about quality of life, safety nets, and other structural issues related to poverty. The coalition between business and the Religious Right has successfully focused the political debate on the more individualistic, business-friendly issues to the exclusion of government initiatives to change the game in the interest of enhancing equality.[18]

The cost of getting elected and the role of big business in underwriting the campaign costs as a way in which American business has come to dominate the federal government's agenda cannot be underestimated. In this connection, the scandal of unregulated "soft money" is even more profound than previously recognized. These are unregulated contributions to state and local parties for general registration and mobilization activities, which can be used for media advertisements that do not actually mention candidates' names. The amount contributed to national parties in the 2000 election totaled a staggering $487 million, for which the politicians' paybacks are inevitable. Indeed the contributions themselves may have been paybacks for services previously rendered. A *Time* magazine study revealed in 1998 that the federal government was shelling out

$125 billion per year to businesses, either by handing out lucrative government contracts or by offering tax annuities to businesses that locate in certain areas or sell their products overseas.[19] That keeping business flourishing has become the business of government today is also evident in the financial bailout that Congress and the Bush administration provided the airlines when travel plummeted after the events of September 11. It is said that the Bipartisan Campaign Reform Act of 2002 will address these abuses. But as we shall subsequently note, the new law alone will not eliminate all the abuses.

In the same spirit, present American tax policies that involve continuing to borrow from the Social Security fund to pay present government expenses has been necessitated by the lower tax rates, especially those for the rich. Though the policy of "borrowing" from the Social Security fund may have its origins in Keynesian economic attempts to spend our way out of debt, today's policies seem more reflective of a narcissist, pro-business preoccupation with the present at the expense of the future.[20] Likewise, as we will note subsequently in some detail, present crusades against affirmative action policies and for funding faith-based helping organizations relate to the business ethos of our era and its links to the emergence of the "new racism."

Shrinking Government: The Reasons

Almost everyone wants smaller government these days. The reasons are related to our cynicism about the electoral process, but other factors are also involved.

The eminent American historian and social critic Christopher Lasch contrasted the political turmoil of the 1960s with our present retreat to purely personal preoccupations. Psychic self-improvement, getting in touch with feelings, and gaining a sense of self-respect occupies most middle- and upper-class Americans more than do concerns with justice. In Lasch's view our narcissist and therapeutic cultural ethos has led most Americans to give up on the possibility of genuine political solutions.[21] But that is not the whole story.

We tend to celebrate the free market and contend that we no longer need Affirmative Action or the assured safety net that welfare used to provide, because once just structures are in place we believe that the basically decent American people will not distort them to their own advantage. Besides, America is a nation of equal opportunity in which everyone can succeed if they work hard enough. The naïveté of such suppositions has been shown statistically by the growing gap between rich and poor. Justice will have a lot better chance in American society if we become more realistic and Augustinian.

This set of attitudes has led to increased suspicion of big government, a preference for small government at the federal level, and the feeling that local government can function more effectively in dealing with social problems. The Augustine in me does not want to dispute totally these observations. Big-government initiatives are by no means the panacea that the Great Society era sometimes suggested that they might be. Whenever there is a monopoly, as sometimes has happened and still happens in federal social programs, a kind of arrogance and bureaucracy develops that either does not truly address the needs of individuals or addresses very inefficiently. The abuses of the welfare system and how it unwittingly created a culture of dependency cannot be denied even by liberal proponents of a welfare safety net.

On the other hand, the idea that local governments and local charities, along with a lot of individual responsibility, are the answer to all our social problems reflects the Enlightenment optimism that precludes Augustinian-constitutional realism. Recall that the whole point of a strong federal government, according to Madison, was that precisely because the federal system is so large, the solutions that evolve through are less likely to reflect only the agenda of some faction or even of an unruly majority. Special-interest agendas are more likely to dominate in solutions of local governing bodies if not checked by the federal government. That critique has been effectively silenced in our present therapeutic, pro-business political ethos.

Another agenda that the silencing of the Augustinian view of human nature has effectively foreclosed is the raising of questions about the pro-business prejudices of government in the post-Reagan era. When these points are raised by certain Democrats, the chorus is sure to be, "Enough of this class-war rhetoric." (The implication is that such concerns are inherently Marxist, which has no credibility in our post–cold war era.) Besides, our celebrity/business culture predisposes us to honor the rich.[22]

Class tensions are also not in the best interests of a free-market economy. Trade functions efficiently only when participants share a common culture. International corporations not only coerce the relativizing of national boundaries but also pressure for an end to appreciating class distinctions, because in reality and in ideology capitalism promotes the ideal of social mobility.[23] Rather than silencing class distinctions, the Constitution in fact reminds us that a competition among factions, often occasioned by an unequal distribution of property or wealth, is to be expected, is part of the human condition.[24] If we silence public debate between these factions, the most powerful of them always wins. To fail to raise questions about how the poor and the working class are being exploited by present government policies is "unconstitutional."

Shrinking Government: Its Implications for Poverty in America

We have previously noted that although the years since 1993 have been good economic times, that has been the case only for some of us (especially for the rich). According to U.S. government statistics, the proportion of American households making more than $75,000 per year has more than doubled in the last three decades (from 10 percent of American families in 1970 to 22.6 percent in 1999). And it is true that the percentage of American families making under $10,000 decreased slightly (about three percentage points from 1970 to 1999). Yet in the same period, the percentage of American families making only $10,000 to $14,000 remained unchanged. The number of working poor has not diminished. In fact, recent statistics indicate that many are poorer. From 1979 to 1997, the income of the lowest-earning 20 percent of Americans dropped from an average of $10,900 to $10,800 annually.

Circumstances for the poor have become even more dire in the economic downturns of the present Bush era. Homelessness is said to have risen by 13 percent nationally. In twenty-five to twenty-seven cities studied by the U.S. Conference of Mayors, emergency food requests were up an average of 23 percent.[25]

As we shrink government, we cut taxes. Of course, money is still required for some services, and with the stress on education, state governments are seeking to enhance their education systems, not least of all by increasing college enrollments. After all, an educated workforce is good for business, and besides, we need to train more teachers to alleviate the teacher shortage. Scholarships would help, but the elite are not interested in more taxes. The "answer"? Gambling. The poor play the lotteries more often, and so they wind up paying for the education of middle-class kids whose parents haven't saved enough in our live-for-the-present, narcissist ethos.

We need also to consider how the poor contribute to business in another way—the prison industry. Is it not peculiar that the jail population has grown since the Reagan years to a record 6.47 million in 2000, especially with poor inmates? In fact, it is hardly surprising that the poor and excluded would turn to crime (in disproportionate numbers among Native Americans and inner-city African Americans). With no viable possibility of living the (narcissist) American dream they see portrayed regularly in the media, the poor may seek to seize it any way it takes—including by criminal means. Besides, the prison industry needs inmates, so there seems to be little incentive for government to seek to improve the conditions of the neighborhoods from which most criminals hail.

In the best tradition of an Augustinian view of government, I must reiterate that the system of a government safety net for all the poor was not without problems. Not only did this system unwittingly create a culture of dependency among many of the impoverished, but such tax money also sustained bureaucratic self-aggrandizement, which has effectively compromised the neighborhood spirit of many impoverished neighborhoods. However, the alternative is not all that attractive.

Advocates of small government forget that private organizations and neighborhood groups were not that successful prior to the establishment of the American welfare system. The proponents of small government also overlook how the concupiscent nature of human beings leads them to pick favorites (those who are most pleasing to their personal tastes). Thus, in unbureaucratic, informal systems of welfare to the poor, some impoverished people (the ones we like and find worthy) are likely to get more than others. The purpose of a bureaucracy is to establish and administer just norms so that all are treated equally. Of course, present administrative standards of welfare can always discriminate. But at least these rubrics are public (unlike informal neighborhood acts of gratuity) and so in principle can be criticized and challenged. When it comes to examining government responsibility for the poor, we need to get some Augustinian realism and not forget the founders' advocacy of creating economic safety nets for the poor.

The End of Affirmative Action

The racial gap is still quite evident. The well-known Gallup poll of public attitudes toward the O. J. Simpson verdict evidences this. According to the April/May 1996 poll, only 24 percent of Whites thought it had been a correct verdict; 73 percent of Blacks agreed with the outcome.[26] The same gap was evident almost one year later regarding whether the United States should offer an official apology for slavery. Only 27 percent of the White population favored such action; 66 percent of the African-American public supported it.[27] The movement for reparations for African Americans for slavery will probably further widen the racial gap.

Yes, the problem of racial profiling by police is at least on the political radar screen. But after several years of talk, why is it still happening, even in the suburbs of a racially progressive metropolis like Atlanta? Given these realities and the realities of Black poverty, the facts that 60 percent of the prison population is African American and that 44 percent of those aged 10–17 are Black (though African-American youth make up only 15 percent of that population) make diabolical common sense.

The Gallup 2001 Social Audit on Black/White relations was even more striking with regard to the gap between the way Blacks and Whites view the world. Sixty-six percent of African Americans believed race will always be a problem in America, while only 45 percent of the White population agreed. Only 9 percent of the African-American population believed that Blacks and Whites are treated alike. A much higher 38 percent of Whites believed that this is already a reality. With regard to treatment by police, 66 percent of the Blacks surveyed believed that Blacks are treated unfairly. Only 35 percent of Whites surveyed agreed.

Other relevant data should be cited. Most recent government statistics indicate that the median family income was $44,000 for Whites but only $28,000 for Black families (though that disparity may be related to a larger number of Black single-parent families). U.S. Department of Labor statistics released in 1998 revealed that over 20 percent of the working poor are African American, while African Americans constitute only about 12 percent of the population. Government statistics in 1999 indicated that 10 percent of the White population fell below the poverty line, while nearly 24 percent of the African-American population and 21 percent of the Native-American/Eskimo population were of that status.[28]

Statistics issued by the Equal Opportunity Commission are no better. In 1999 African Americans made up 14 percent of the American labor force, but only 6.2 percent of the managers were Black, and only 6.6 percent were professionals. By contrast, Whites constituted 71.6 percent of the labor force but held 86.3 percent of the managerial positions and 81.8 percent of the professional positions. A White person is more likely to hold a managerial or professional job than to be a laborer. It is just the opposite for Black Americans. White men are the big winners, as they constitute 38.4 percent of the labor force but hold 58.5 percent of managerial positions and 40.6 percent of the professional positions. White women lag far behind in obtaining management positions, holding only 27.8 percent of such positions while holding nearly as large a percentage of jobs in the labor force as do their male counterparts (33.2 percent of the jobs). Granted, women do hold a slightly higher percentage of the professional positions than do men nationwide (51 percent to 49 percent), but when we note that teachers and nurses are grouped under the category of "professional" the gains are perhaps less impressive.[29]

The small-government ethos of our day and our social narcissism make it highly unlikely that the federal government will undertake any new, massive effort to change race relations. Of course, Clinton raised the issue and (as did George W. Bush) appointed some well-placed African Americans in prestigious positions. But most of it was talk, mere symbolism. Other dynamics, some related to the business ethos, also account for the new racism.

It has been in the interests of business and their political lackeys to stir racial animosities, not because they are blatant racists, but because it is in their interests for maintaining power. Contempt for the Black poor in our changing economy is a way of helping the middle class see that it has wealth and power. Despite its declining fortunes, at least it has it a lot better than some groups, and the purported reason the White middle class has it better is that they have "worked harder."[30] This is another reason that the new racism has emerged.

The decline of the American city, coupled with dynamics of African-American leadership, has further exacerbated racial tensions. The heritage of Black Power and nationalist propensities is very much alive in the circles of the African-American elite. Even those with empathy for the integrationist strands of Martin Luther King Jr.'s heritage need to remain in dialogue with those involved in the Black Power movement in order to maintain their own credibility. The critique by Marcus Garvey and others of the idea of integration in a society that refuses to practice what it preaches has been globalized into a sweeping critique of Western culture as a whole. In some cases this critique is made not just in the interest of highlighting the unique contributions of Africa and its sons and daughters of the diaspora. Rather, armed with the relativistic philosophies of Immanuel Kant (1724–1804) or deconstructionism, the critique is aimed at foreclosing any possibility of building bridges between White and Black, of finding commonalties.[31]

At such an intellectual level there is little hope of bridging the racial divide. Many White intellectuals react defensively to such thinking. The fact that they react more defensively than occurs in ethnic dialogues with a less complex history, such as the ongoing rivalries among Scandinavian cultures and their mutual influencing of each other, or the debate over whether the impact of Hellenization has been a good thing for the West, leads the observer to wonder whether the heritage of racism is still alive in such virulent critiques. No one gets as upset about Dutch courses taught at Calvin College in Grand Rapids, Michigan, or about the Norwegian cultural courses at St. Olaf College in Minnesota, as they do about Black Studies majors.[32] These dynamics also apply to relations between dominant American society and Native Americans and other minorities. Analogies might also be noted with regard to the gender gap and the sexual preference controversy. (I focus on Black/White relations at this point because this issue has been the most public and to some extent, due to slavery, the most tragic.)

References to controversies over language and culture courses remind us of controversies over bilingual education in the public schools. The English-only faction tends to rely on a nativism that aims to defend distinct American values from a nihilistic relativism perceived as implicit in the push for bilingualism.

With regard to the state of the American city and how it has exacerbated the new racism, the dynamics are analogous to what has happened at the intellectual level. Increasingly, urban trends are making it harder and harder for Black and White to find common ground.

The city of the nineteenth century and the first half of the twentieth century was a paradoxical mix of the (often ethnic) neighborhood and the cosmopolitan city. One never was too far away from the high culture (and sometimes loose living) of an America in which one's ethnic origin ultimately melted. Yet at the same time, the neighborhood was just across town or over the river. In the city, it was not hard to be ethnic and American at the same time. Outside the neighborhood, its diverse citizens shared a lot in common, and sometimes went to school together and worked together, without ceasing to be Irish, Italian, Jewish, Dutch, Norwegian, Chinese, or African back in the neighborhood.

In this context there was much goodwill toward race relations on all sides in the decades following World War II. Even ethnic neighborhoods, for all their anxiety about losing their particularity if new immigrants and Blacks started moving in, remained committed to the principles of fair play that they believed their new country stood for. (To this day, many of these White ethnics know that it is not Blacks and Hispanics who are causing them problems.) Jackie Robinson's legacy in Brooklyn was very much alive and contributing to these feelings of commonality and the need for justice. Economic pressure for integration began to be exerted in the South at the outset of the Civil Rights movement.

White social reformers committed to the cause of integration and social justice made some mistakes in the 1960s by advocating and successfully engineering assaults on the urban ethnic neighborhood as somehow embodying racism (as if you could not be a friend of the African-American cause and still prefer to live among your fellow Irish or Italians). Cities began to change as businesses went elsewhere, because the mills either closed or were relocated and what replaced them (finance, communications, real estate, tourism, entertainment) did not provide jobs for the masses. Poverty began to hit the ethnic neighborhoods, both Black and White. The White flight, which had begun with the first wave of business relocations, followed with even more force. As the neighborhoods deteriorated, even those with jobs in the city moved to the suburbs. What is left? Poverty.

More recently we are observing the phenomena of the yuppies returning to the city and the revitalizing of neighborhoods. But it is not the old ethnic neighborhood in which the new urban citizen is living. The old neighborhood apartments and tenements have been revitalized or replaced with rich condominiums whose rental costs and real estate value effectively drive the old residents out. Meanwhile, the poor Black neighborhoods and the old immigrant communities are increasingly poor and isolated. Fewer and fewer opportunities are provided for those in the "hood" to go into the city, since there are no jobs there and less chance to qualify for one of the elite city schools. (Only in the new immigrant communities, especially the Asian neighborhoods, populated by those who have high enough levels of education or who place enough emphasis on education that they qualify for the few good jobs left in the city, is this cycle of isolation broken so that they participate in the old mix of being able to share in the common urban culture while remaining ethnic.)

Just as the dynamics of the academic world make it harder and harder for Blacks and Whites to share and celebrate a common culture, so it is in the city. The isolation breeds more suspicion and more racism. Note how the real racial tension in the cities, the real source of poverty, then, is not between old-line, middle-class, ethnic White residents and African Americans. It is occasioned by a business cycle, exacerbated by opportunistic racial politics we have noted, that is effectively isolating these segments from each other. (Analogous, though distinct, dynamics have a similar effect on race relations in the suburbs. A combination of real estate dynamics—the decline of property values in White neighborhoods when minorities begin to move in—and the homogeneous and transient character of modern suburbia entails that Black and White do not get to know each other and so rarely share a sense of community. Generally speaking, they do not worship together either.) A healthy dose of Augustinian suspicion about human institutions might alert the public to how its latest racial agonies are to a great extent functions of good old-fashioned greed. Those oppressed by the latest capitalist bounties have a lot in common after all.[33]

Civil Rights in a New (Individualistic) Mode

Narcissist and business trends have combined to transform the civil rights heritage in striking, sometimes disturbing ways. We have become a notoriously litigious society. We will sue over anything, even frivolous matters. Even those in favor of small government want government protection if it helps them. Augustine could have told us that. We will always seek to do what will help us the most, even if it is at cross-purposes with what we previously said we believe.

For examples of idiotic, frivolous lawsuits, consider those mounted by White professors at African-American institutions like Livingstone College in North Carolina who cry about discrimination from the victims of racism when White colleagues in such institutions with an ounce of integrity know full well that they serve on behalf of the will of the Black community and what best serves African-American interests. Thus if Black scholars can be found to replace White faculty, these interests are best served. White academics in these settings knew or should have known the rules of the game before they started playing. They agreed to these rules before taking their jobs. Their suits are a bit like a ballplayer suing the league for being called out on three strikes. As for frivolity, consider how some Americans now sue eating establishments like McDonald's because the coffee is too hot. Is such an inconvenience really worth legal action?

While the litigation that facilitated the Civil Rights movement was always on behalf of the community, the latest round of suits is not intended to set precedents to benefit the common good. The suits are all about the individual litigant getting his goodies. Individual rights are a key element of narcissism. Of course, lawyers see this as good business. We have already noted how they have bought into the business paradigm. We see this in the legal profession's reducing itself to sponsoring advertisements and getting to the scene of accidents in order to cultivate potential clients in lawsuits. Government structures are not so bad for businesspeople when they help business.

Shrinking Government: Its Implications for Ecology

The influence that big business has on government is apparent in the present administration's ecological policies. George W. Bush has pressed for opening the Bridger-Teton National Forest in Wyoming, as well as the pristine Arctic National Wildlife Refuge in Alaska, to oil and gas drilling. The old oilman still seems to have a lot of friends in the business. (And of course we need the extra energy, right?) But we don't hear much from the "compassionate conservative" about how the bulk of urban pollution gets dumped in poor Black neighborhoods.

In the best traditions of Augustine, I do not want to give the impression that the Clinton administration's more "green-friendly" policies were any less scarred by special interests (he did owe political debts to the environmentalist lobby). A particularly glaring instance of the federal government's failure to consider the common good is evident in Klamath Falls, Oregon, where an irrigation canal was closed off by the Bureau of Reclamation in order to save an endangered species of suckerfish. The result: some 1,400 farmers in the river basin were cut off from irrigation and watched their land dry up. The suckerfish were preserved, while the farmers went bankrupt.[34]

Augustinian Political Common Sense

Given these realities of campaign financing and their impact on government policy, is it any accident that even Democrats are pro-business these days? Shocking? It should be no surprise to the Augustinian.

The Bipartisan Campaign Reform Act of 2002 seeks to address these abuses. However, it is by no means uncontroversial and is not the final solution. The law is primarily an amendment to the Federal Election Campaign Act of 1971, which forbade corporations and unions from contributing to federal elections, while also limiting the contributions of individuals and PACs. The new law seeks to close the 1971 legislation's so-called soft-money loophole. According to the 1971 law, exemptions on contributions are made if contributions are given to state and local party committees for general voter registration or mobilization activities. In other words, you can give all you want to the local parties, and they can use it for media advertisements as long as the message merely urges hearers to vote for the party and does not expressly portray advocacy of the party's candidate for the presidency. We all know of instances in which such advertisements connoted support for the candidate without actually mentioning his name. This soft-money loophole has effectively negated the 1971 law. The last federal election illustrates this, as almost $500 million was contributed directly to candidates this way.

The Bipartisan Campaign Reform Act seeks to close this loophole by placing very specific strictures on how such contributions might be used, strictures that preclude the use of such soft money for any public communication that specifically names a candidate for federal office (Sec. 323). Another way it tightens up contribution limits is political ads that outside groups can run in the month or two before the election (Sec. 201).

Questions must be raised about these well-intentioned provisions. Besides the problem of whether campaign financing limits encroach on First Amendment free-speech rights, since no provision is made to reduce actual campaign expenditures those with special political interests (unions, corporations, well-landed individuals) will still find a way to exert influence. Instead of feeding soft money to the parties, these contributors are likely to make their own independent ads. Consequently, it is not surprising that in the first year after the new campaign legislation was enacted, a number of businesses began forming Political Action Committees (PACs) to circumvent the law. Such PACs became the entity these companies used to allocate money for political advertisements that otherwise would have gone to the national political parties. These PACs can function as the means for big business to continue to keep politicians in their pockets through threats or promises of political ads and advocacy that might help or hurt the officeholder.

Another problem with the new legislation is its Republican bias. It unfairly targets unions by trying to forbid their spending on political activities with mandated payments by workers who are union members but who may not share the leadership's commitments. Overlooked (deliberately) is the fact that many workers in a corporation may not share its management's political propensities, yet the bill still allows the total assets of such corporations to be available for political lobbying efforts. Is there a fairer way to facilitate campaign finance reform?

In my view, we need to create a dynamic that reduces campaign expenditures. But how to do that? A 1976 Supreme Court decision threw out earlier legislation that had sought to limit how much a candidate for federal office could spend, while the limits on how much could be raised stayed in place. As a result, we have our present situation of rich political novices being elected to Congress because they can privately fund their campaigns at higher levels than their less wealthy rivals.

Since setting limits on campaign spending is not an option, what we need to do is find a way to make campaigns cost less. It does not take a political scientist to address this matter. The major costs in today's political campaigns are the media advertisements. Is there a way to reduce these costs and to level the playing field? Could the Federal Communications Commission or congressional legislation create incentives for the networks to provide free prime-time exposure or advertisements to all candidates and to refuse to accept paid ads?[35]

This proposal of free media access for candidates for office does not solve all the problems associated with ethics and politics. An Augustinian is ever aware of the imperfections and short-sightedness of legislative proposals and political agendas. It may be that in the foreseeable future, with the increased use of the Internet, efforts to legislate free media access by candidates may not be required, as more and more campaigns will find that websites and e-mail messages to voters suffice for media exposure. Perhaps this new technology will solve the problems caused by skyrocketing campaign costs. Although it is too late for the 2002 midterm election, do we not need something in place for the 2004 presidential elections?

Forgive my pessimism (or is it Augustinian/constitutional realism?), but the idea of limiting campaign costs by pressuring networks may not be politically viable for the foreseeable future. In fact, the entire subject of ethics and politics is not on the radar screen of most Americans. A January 2001 Gallup poll revealed that only 7 percent of the American public regarded government as the most important problem in our country today.

On the other hand, the poll did indicate that 13 percent of the public identified ethics/morality/religion/family decline as the most important problem in the country.[36] As such, this set of issues received the highest ranking in the poll as a problem for Americans. Perhaps we could expand this popular yearning for morality into a movement for campaign finance reform on grounds that the public morality of our political leaders needs to set the tone for a revival of American morality.

Even if this appeal to morality in politics were made, it would likely succeed only if undertaken with an Augustinian spirit. The public needs to be made aware that, given what we are, people will always cater to what will serve their self-interests. Quite naturally, politicians will do what it takes to get elected, or at least to earn a distinguished legacy; there is no reason to be shocked about it. Ways need to be found to make concern for interests other than those that dominate today a bit more attractive to the politicians. Political common sense, rather than merely lamenting the evils of the system or lecturing on values, is the way to go. And we have a political system, despite all its flaws, that can allow this new agenda to come about if we find compelling ways to attract and pressure the politicians.

If we could get the public to endorse the Augustinian view of human persons, we could make our appeal to politicians not so much on the basis of partisan politics, but simply by urging that given our selfishness, we need to take care that all of America's interests are balanced. If we do not, the most powerful and wealthy will exploit everyone else. Until Americans return to these constitutional roots, and stop thinking everyone is good, we will go on naively believing that everything going on in America is just fine (and it is just fine, for those of us who are profiting from it now). Augustine can straighten us out, and make us more sensitive to the interests of the poor, the disenfranchised, and even the squeezed middle class.

four

A Business-Driven Society

Whatever Happened to a Real Quality of Life?

Later historians will surely characterize our era as crazed with economic preoccupations, perhaps no less than the 1920s. Of the few heroes Americans have, successful business leaders are among the most prominent. Americans, most notably Baby Boomers, are almost one-dimensionally focused on career and financial security.

Getting ahead economically has always been the American way. But the refrain of the 1992 Clinton campaign still has resonance in the American psyche: "It's the economy, stupid!" We have already observed how single-mindedly government has devoted itself to the business agenda. Certainly, the hours Americans put in on the job are indicative of this obsessive devotion to business. According to 1999 U.S. Bureau of Labor statistics, over 25 million Americans work 49 hours or more each week. Nearly 12 percent of the workforce is on the job between 49 and 59 hours weekly, and 11 million (or 8.5 percent) put in over 60 hours.[1] For these Americans, there ain't much time for anything but business.

Except for some decline of confidence in the wake of the 2002 Enron, WorldCom, and ImClone financial chicaneries, big-business entrepreneurs have become and remain the new American folk heroes. Even if they do not quite trust their business leaders, most American still want to emulate them. For example, though Bill Gates may have his enemies, as recently as April 2002 a Gallup poll indicated that 79 percent of the American public approves of Microsoft. A March 1999 poll found that the public even approved of Gates personally (59 percent approval vs. 18 percent disapproval).[2] Business models even permeate religious organizations and educational institutions (as will be discussed in later chapters). Likewise, analysts have lamented how sports have become more business-oriented—even NCAA Division I college sports (as the Knight Commission, seeking to bring about reform of the system, has lamented).

Business-Driven Athletics

The introduction of free agency in professional sports certainly fits the new cultural climate. Major leaguers are now prime examples of the "flexible" high-powered labor force. The price has been outlandishly high salaries, paid for by once-loyal fans with skyrocketing ticket costs. The cost of such free agency has also emerged in the loss of fan loyalty to teams, especially among the younger generations. You will not find so many young Atlantans who will stick by the Braves, sink or swim, the way that I knew loyal Dodger and Yankee fans in Brooklyn and the rest of New York did in my youth.

The Augustine in me hastens to remind us that the old system of binding contracts, which made players property of the team that originally signed them for life unless traded, was heavily rigged in the owners' favor. The old system, then, seemed stacked in favor of the owners. Player salaries were incredibly low by today's standards. Today's rookie receives double what Mickey Mantle and Willie Mays received forty years ago. But middle-class families could still afford reserved seats in Yankee Stadium, and team loyalty was a way of life. Baseball and other professional sports became integrated under the old system, and until O'Malley pulled the Dodgers out of Brooklyn, which system best served the common good?

As the new millennium began, we even found ourselves treating child athletes as pampered free agents. Amateur Athletic Union (AAU) basketball teams and traveling youth baseball teams recruit children from all over the country in some cases. These children are totally free agents who can choose to play for whomever they wish with no regard for regional loyalty or the opportunity to play with friends. One traveling baseball team in the Atlanta area (the Woolsey Yankees) recruits twelve-year-olds from all over the South to play one hundred games per year. Why? So these kids have a chance to win a scholarship, if not to make the major leagues. The cost? Youth baseball is no longer for the fun of it. It's preparation for a career. The ever-present business model again prevails.

These dynamics, the importance for parental ego that their children excel in sports, coupled with the narcissist propensity to live through our children's accomplishments (for they are little more than extensions of our egos), account for the outrageous behavior of many parents at youth sports events. Children are regularly berated by parents at such events, and sometimes the adults even fight each other.

New International Dynamics: Globalization

The new business-related dynamics have been exacerbated by the nature of the post-industrial economy of the post–Cold War computer era. In a sense, current economic developments contribute to the Americans' growing disinterest in their government. Governmental structures and institutions have progressively less influence on the economy. Economics has become so internationalized, so much the domain of the multinational corporation, that national political leaders are no longer capable of controlling economic trends. This helps explain America's recent post-Reagan dissatisfaction with the Roosevelt heritage of a managed economy in favor of the presently prevailing philosophy of free and open markets.

The economic theory of the Roosevelt heritage, indebted to the eminent economist John Maynard Keynes, advocated spending our way out of debt. This strategy presupposes that the increase in demand will enhance business, whose growth, insofar as it is a partner in society, will enhance the common good.[3] Champions of the free market presume the good citizenship of American corporations.[4] But multinational corporations will not necessarily function as collective citizens in a society and formulate strategies that reflect any sense of obligation to the common good of that society. In fact, the multinational corporation, run as it is by today's professional managers, is likely to take the money and run for the latest short-term profit. Indeed, an Augustinian conception of human nature would remind us that corporations will never be good citizens unless compelled to be by legislation and the tax structure.

If the unprohibited free market will not unequivocally serve the common good of the nation in our new economic ethos, the old Keynesian-Roosevelt model has its flaws as well in the new context. Its strategy of raising taxes to pay off the national debt so that inflation is reduced, which in turn will increase the value of investors' holdings, in order that increased production by American-owned corporations might be encouraged, is also a practical impossibility. The various interest groups in American society, each identifying the national interest with its own concerns, veto that approach. The unwillingness of all interest groups to lower expectations in order to reap long-term benefits may be a manifestation of the impact of the new therapeutic consciousness on contemporary American society. But more likely such attitudes bespeak modern America's distorted appropriation of the myth of progress associated with the Enlightenment. The Clinton and Bush administrations' and the educational establishment's near unequivocal confidence in the benefits of the new knowledge technologies suggest these attitudes. None of the available models for making the economy work serve the interests of America and of most Americans!

As the greatest world superpower, business has become more influential in shaping national and international trends than national governments. Big businesses are international, having no loyalty to particular political entities. Thus what drives many international and national decisions is not what is best for the common good, but what is good for business. Some analysts have concluded as a result that a world of porous borders is being created by these dynamics, which will lead to the atrophy of the ability of nations to define themselves as distinct entities.[5]

We can understand the European Union and its drive to establish a common European currency as well as other free-trade pacts in this light. Another recent example of this business-driven globalization is the International Olympic Committee's decision to award the 2008 games to Beijing. Human rights groups were outraged, and the decision is not necessarily in the interests of Western democracies. But the celebrations at Coca-Cola, United Parcel Service, and McDonald's (all of which, by the way, have either been major Olympic sponsors in the past or promise to be) were joyous, as CEOs of the companies envisioned all sorts of new business opportunities.[6]

The new internationalizing, globalizing tendencies that erode national borders are not greeted with universal acclaim. While they seem to diminish differences and antagonisms among states, some backlash is inevitable, especially from those segments of the global population that are being left behind by the new economy or have never felt that they were equal partners with the players forming the new global economy. Consequently, some of the most recent outbreaks of nationalism—like the ethnic conflicts in the former Yugoslavia, the Protestant-Catholic conflicts in Northern Ireland, Pan-Africanism, and the terrorism inspired by Islamic fundamentalism that swept across the eastern United States on September 11, 2001—might be understood as reactions to the monolithic drives of business to level national and regional distinctions, as these ethnic groups feel they are being swallowed up in the new global society without their contributions to the coalition or their interests being taken seriously.[7]

Other Significant Business Trends in the New Economy

An unprecedented number of women have joined the American labor force during the past three decades. In 1970, 31.3 million women were employed. That number swelled to 54.8 million in 1999.[8]

This development has been good for business. The degree to which it is good for society as a whole is a matter on which to elaborate in subsequent chapters. With regard to its benefits for business, we should note that the larger labor force created by more women working outside the home means less need to lure a smaller male labor force with higher salaries. We must not rule out the relationship between the rise of feminism and the dominance of big business in American society.

In addition, some advertising has been geared to women's liberation, as women's economic liberation created a broader market. One thinks of the old Virginia Slims cigarette ad, "You've come a long way, baby."[9] Women now even have their own cable television network, with appropriate advertising geared to this market.

The cornerstone of modern management practice is the belief that loose networks are more open to decisive reinvention than are pyramidal hierarchies.[10] This has led to a stress on teams and teamwork to deal with short-term tasks. It has also meant the need for fewer administrators, which in turn leads to downsizing and to more administrative responsibilities for the remaining workforce. Leaders in this style of doing business need to be able to let go of the past and accept fragmentation.[11] These are realities of today's business world.

Another characteristic of today's business-management strategies is to favor short-term profits over long-term stability. The thinking here is that the market is more consumer-driven, so dynamic as to mandate that business can never do the same thing year after year.[12] However, it became clear to many business leaders by the mid-1990s that constant reinvention of companies was not good business. The American Management Association even showed in studies that downsizings lead to lower profits and declining worker productivity. That is not surprising, since morale and motivation of workers suffer under these conditions.

This leads to the question of why downsizing and corporate reorganization are so much in vogue. It has to do with the market. Investors tend to regard such reorganizations as desirable, and so the stock prices rise. Thus, although the administrative disruptions may not be justifiable in the long term, the short-term returns to stockholders are strong incentives.[13] And since the mid-1980s, when a radical change in the stock market made hostile takeovers a constant threat to business managers, short-term profits to ward off such takeovers became a management way of life.[14] The big losers in this trend have been those in electronics and computers, constituting 20 percent of the 677,000 laid off in 1998, a figure 10 percent higher than the U.S. economy's previous high in 1993 (at the end of the recession that doomed the senior Bush's administration).[15]

Fear of job loss leads to a psychologically unhealthy sense of always needing to start over. No coherent life narrative that provides happy, well-adjusted people with a meaning and plan for life can truly develop in such a transitory ethos. In short, apart from a realistic, transcendent faith perspective, people will not find much wholeness and happiness in a transitory business climate like ours.[16]

The New Economy and the Exploitation of the Labor Force

The business dynamics described above have taken a toll on the American public. The International Survey Research Corporation found in 1994 that 44 percent of employees surveyed from a variety of corporations believed their workloads were excessive. A 1994 survey by the American Management Association revealed that 51 percent of those surveyed cited "frustration" and 49.4 percent cited "stress" as the best ways to characterize their feelings about the workday. More than 40 percent of professional and clerical workers surveyed by Gallup complained about stress on the job.[17] No wonder: a summer 2001 Gallup poll revealed that nearly one-fourth of the workforce feared an upcoming layoff.

The pressures on the American labor force are intense. It has already been noted that in 1999 the Bureau of Labor Statistics revealed that over 25 million Americans work more than 49 hours per week and that significant numbers in the American labor force work more than 60 hours weekly. This represents a significant increase since 1980, when only 11.2 percent of the workforce put in 49–59 hours on the job, and only 7.9 percent put in more than 60 hours weekly.[18] In fact, a study by a United Nations agency, the International Labor Organization, revealed that Americans work nearly 49.5 weeks per year (increasing 36 hours per year in the 1990s). As a result, Americans average 1,978 working hours per year, 100 hours (about 2.5 weeks) more than do the Japanese and 500 hours (12.5 weeks) more than the British.

Internal corporate pressure in our increasingly tight job market supports the new stress on more hours, fewer vacations, and higher levels of productivity. As a result, new pressures have inevitably been placed on family life.[19] The new capitalism not only promotes compulsive work. It also nurtures a contempt for "useless" intellectual pursuits.[20]

We need to look at the nature of teamwork in the new corporate America, because it has implications for understanding the present economy's inequality, the dissatisfaction of many workers, and the way in which our present business ethos feeds the narcissism of our day. The team is a group of people assembled for a specific short-term task; it is not a community with a tradition. The good team player is flexible, always willing to work with a new set of characters. Thus, detachment is essential for getting ahead in business today.

Because there is no sense of communal traditions, seniority counts for less and less in corporate America. As a result, there is a prejudice in favor of youthful workers over those with experience. The number of workers 55 to 65 dropped from nearly 80 percent of the American labor force in 1970 to 65 percent in 1990.[21] This prejudice against age and experience fits the ethos of instant gratification of a narcissist outlook, especially as marketed and popularized by the media.

The good team player also must be a good listener, willing to share everything with the team, and not give the appearance of exercising authority. Stress is placed on people skills (i.e., the ability to manipulate appearances and the behavior of others). Good team players are also good actors, manipulating others into wrongly believing that they are not pulling the strings. These attractive business traits have deep implications for how administrators relate to others. Business mandates friendliness. But it does not encourage in-depth friendships. In fact, the "friendliness" of the office conceals savage competition: "Be nice, in order to get what you want. But if someone's been nice to you, watch your butt."[22]

The sort of detachment and superficial cooperation that the new paradigm of teamwork encourages is an attractive characteristic for workers in the new economy. Such detachment is necessary in a business climate that demands innovation and re-envisioning. Truly innovative workers in the new labor force refuse to be caught up in past intrigues, and when one is detached from old loyalties it is easier to function in such innovative ways.[23]

The idea implicit in the teamwork model of corporate management—that workers and management are on the same level in the team—is in fact a pro-business fiction. The sort of cooperation that results from such business-management styles is a mask for real feelings. Further, the resulting interpersonal style results in a mask of friendliness to customers not necessarily accompanied by a commitment truly to serve them.[24]

American sociologist Richard Sennett has observed that these dynamics of the workplace produce an ironic personality. According to philosopher Richard Rorty, such an ironic personality is one always aware of contingency in all aspects of life. Without any certainties, the ironic office worker is likely to reject or walk away from all long-term commitments (since they are known to be ultimately contingent even when they are entered into under the guise of permanency) and so is ultimately alone.[25] All that is left is the solitary self and the quest for self-fulfillment.

The new business-management version of teamwork exploits the worker. It seems to reduce the natural adversarial relationship between labor and management, which is always healthy in a democratic society where each side has its own interests. Of course, in a society where we think people are fundamentally good, such conflict is distasteful, and the idea of a team takes care of it. The reality is, though, that management gains even more power in this arrangement. When workers try to protest pro-management moves or seek decisions in their own interests, the specter of their being bad team players is raised. Under the cloak of teamwork, management effectively silences their protests and resistance. Likewise, the boss is better able to protect his or her interests in this model, because when things do not work out the boss is not held accountable, since the workers had a voice in the failed decision.

Another team dynamic is that it can subtly undermine the value of seniority (just what today's flexible business wants). On the team, the senior worker must share all that he or she knows with colleagues. Knowledge is power. But once the knowledge garnered by one with a thirty-year career is commonly known in a company, even by new hires, the older worker is replaceable, even expendable, when downsizing happens. After all, you can pay the new hire less.[26]

The widespread use of new computer technologies, including the cell phone, gives the appearance of lightening routine tasks. But what they effectively do is exacerbate patterns of overwork, as they create an ethos in which managers can legitimately be expected and expect those responsible to them to bring their jobs home and work 24/7. Supervision of workers, even to the point of gaining insight about their personal lives, is made more readily possible with the new technology.[27] Far from enhancing American life, the new economy has effectively lowered the standard of living. It has also impacted American life in other, no less troubling, ways.

Institutional Impact of the New Economy

As a result of the dynamics described, labor unions have fallen on hard times. Most white-collar workers have never been unionized, and harsh employment realities have not led to much successful labor organization.[28] Statistics tell the story of the decline in organized labor. In 1983, 20.1 percent of America's salaried and wage workers were union members. By 2001, only 14 percent held such membership.[29]

In some respects the decline of the labor union movement is related to the new style of business-management techniques, with its stress on "teamwork," which makes it harder for the labor force to defend its rights and to confront management with concerns. As noted, in the context of such teamwork, whenever a worker raises concerns or when workers try to organize, the suggestion is made that they are not real team players. In this context, unions are either effectively banned or made "politically incorrect" in the company's ethos.

These dynamics have made it possible for managers to keep operating expenses low, as workers are not readily able to lobby for higher wages, benefits, and a shorter work week. In fact, keeping operating expenses low was the key factor in the business boom of the 1990s.[30] Indeed, management is now so much in control of the social agenda that it is able to package layoffs as good for business (as "downsizing") when in fact layoffs are a sign of management's miscalculations and failures.[31]

We have already noted how the rich are getting richer and the poor, poorer. That the squeeze is on the middle class is evident in statistics reported about the economy from 1992 through 1998. The economy grew 3.6 percent annually during these years. But the average worker's wages grew only 3 percent annually. (And that increase was not shared equally.) At the same time, the increase in consumer spending, fueled both by cost-of-living increases and by a narcissistic need for instant gratification, increased 5.3 percent annually.[32]

In other words, the rate of increase in spending nearly doubled that of the increase in wages. No one can save much for retirement or for the kids' college accounts at that pace. The middle class is clearly being squeezed.

Other statistics paint a similarly grim portrait. From 1988 through 1998, family incomes for the nation's middle class rose an average of $780. The top 5 percent of American family incomes gained $50,760.[33] White-collar males earned $19.24

per hour in 1997. When the 1973 salary is calculated for inflation increase, the 1997 average represents only a six-cents-per-
hour increase over 1973 wages. Even among such professionals as lawyers, doctors, and university professors, there is
similar wage stagnation. The only category exempt from these
wage pressures has been that of chief executive officers of corporations, whose salary plus bonuses grew by a whopping 44.6
percent from 1989 through 1997.[34]

Related to these dynamics has been the decline in pension
funds. While in 1979 companies were contributing 63 cents per
hour worked to their employees' pensions funds, the contributions level dropped to 45 cents by 1996.[35] These companies
also seem to be cutting back on health insurance for workers
as they shift to managed-care plans. Recent government statistics compiled by the Census Bureau indicate that 44 million
Americans have no health insurance. Earlier reports had indicated that this was true of 18 percent of the workforce.[36]

The increased cost-of-living expenses experienced by American workers has been exacerbated by other dynamics. We have
already noted how management's prioritizing of short-term
gains has helped nurture an attitude of "get it right away" in
American society. Such entrepreneurial strategies have filtered
down to or have been reflected in the lives of most Americans,
as record levels of household debt have been recorded. By the
end of 2000 the average consumer had nearly $9,000 in credit-
card debt.[37]

The squeeze felt by the American middle class also accounts
for the revivified new racism in its manifest forms, especially
directed against the Black urban poor. Contempt for the Black
poor is the White middle class's way of denying that they might
be next.[38]

In our pro-business, 24/7 work ethos, government is seen as
the enemy by the flexible corporation. Strong governments are
deemed likely to interfere with corporate reorganizations that
might be to the detriment of less powerful citizens.[39] It seems
impossible to reject the possibility that the sweeping endorsement of such attitudes by Americans, coupled with the data
noted in the preceding chapter regarding how our campaign

finance system entails catering to big donors, can explain a lot of present government policies. A government committed to leaving business alone to do its business because it is indebted to big donors will of course support the tax cuts of the Bush administration, the assault on a graduated income tax, the federal government's generally passive, even encouraging, role during the merger mania of the 1990s, and the availability of government bailout money for the airlines strapped after the September 11, 2001, terrorist episodes. That such pro-business policies are not necessarily for the common good was made woefully evident when the airlines protected by the government proceeded to lay off more than 100,000 employees and was again made evident more recently by the Enron and WorldCom scandals. We need to look at the price that the American psyche and social character have had to pay for these dynamics, for our economic growth at the expense of lifestyle issues.

The New Economy and the Narcissist Personality of Our Time

Work has always played a role in shaping the character of workers, so that different business conditions have nurtured different values and behaviors. Free-market capitalism shaped a new sort of worker. Adam Smith recognized this as early as 1796. He claimed that the market had a dulling effect on people. He also believed, in a very Augustinian manner, that it was a characteristic of humans in general to overrate their abilities, to have overweening conceit.[40]

The implications of the new model of business management for character formation in contemporary American society are even more disturbingly obvious. As previously suggested, the narcissist character does well in this new business environment. The premium on manipulating others, on superficial cooperation and flexibility rather than on long-term commitments and loyalty, is just right for the narcissist lifestyle. Likewise, the insincere people skills required by the team captain and the worker who deals with clients demand the sort of masking of one's true self and the desire to accumulate admirers that typifies narcissism.

The increased use of computers in the workplace also lends to the nurturing of certain character traits that seem less than wholesome when subjected to critical analysis. Intelligence in using machines is dull when the interest is operational rather than self-critical. When I am skilled only in making the machine work, when I am not interested in how the machine affects society and how it might be used differently or when I am not even willing to challenge its use, my expertise is merely routinized and therefore dulled by routine. I do not need to think. I am no longer challenged. I know *how* to do things, not *why* I do them. Computers intensify such dynamics. They provide answers, but not necessarily understanding of the answer provided. I may have the answer from the computer without knowing why it is the right answer.

These dynamics entail that I am detached or removed from the work undertaken on the computer. It is not quite mine. I passively receive data or have the mathematical equation figured out for me. I do not have to do much research myself, save my mastery of the machine. With regard to the actual subject of the problem considered, I am a spectator, not the problem solver.[41]

This sort of fluidity and detachment is precisely what the employer in today's flexible new economy wants in the labor force. These computer-nurtured traits of detachment and lack of personal investment in what one does are also compatible with the narcissist personality, which other dynamics in the modern workplace encourage.

These personality traits do nothing to enhance race relations. The workforce may be more integrated, but Blacks and Whites really do not know each other better, do not socialize together. The teamwork on the job does not involve the sort of relationships that lead to friendship, because loyalty and a shared history get in the way of the flexibility that "good" business demands. Besides, the colleague on my team cannot fully be trusted. The colleague is ultimately a competitor, who if possessing my skills and younger than I, may survive the next downsizing that I don't.

There are other ways in which modern business-management models transform styles of doing business and unwittingly create climates in which narcissist ways of living are subtly encouraged, as the message is given that narcissist traits of flexibility (even with the truth), desire to accumulate admirers, and ability to manipulate people and images are the way to get ahead in life. A number of interpreters of contemporary culture, most notably Alan Wolfe, have lamented that conditional honesty has replaced absolute commitments to truth.[42] If you tell the truth all the time, you can get in trouble on the job. But the successful narcissist operates with the more flexible version of truth. The financial accounting scandals occasioned in 2002 by the false reporting of expenses and exaggeration of corporate earnings by Enron, WorldCom, and others further testify to the contextual character of truth-telling.

It is debatable whether we are less honest today. Americans of every generation have lied about participation in the war of their generation. It is interesting, though, to observe how contextual even our lies now are. Interpreters have noted a surprising increase among Baby Boomers lying about their involvement in Vietnam, as many who were deferred are now claiming to have served. Such an affirmation is one that few Boomers, even those who did in fact serve, would have wanted to proclaim proudly in most public circles in the 1970s or early 1980s.[43]

The team-management model of contemporary business contributes to this ethos of insincerity, of which dishonesty is just one component. In the team, I may disagree with and even dislike my colleague. But except in rare cases, the adversarial style of debate and dispute is discouraged. Of course, this discouragement is also in line with the dominance of the therapeutic mindset in the American social psyche, whose development we have observed. Such pop psychology teaches us that conflict is a bad thing and, that we need to learn to work through it. Of course, when it's the boss with whom you're in conflict or when you know that the boss disapproves of conflict you might be having with a co-worker, the mask on feelings will inevitably emerge. You will not work through the ill feelings. You will just repress them. Team management encourages insincerity, an artificial chuminess, and superficiality in relationships.

Even in the older hierarchical models of business management, workers needed to muzzle their hostility, even if the bosses did not. Yet because longevity in the workplace was the norm, a sense of loyalty to worker and company was in the air; there were more incentives for genuine resolution of ill feelings. Quite often, you came to like and care for the people with whom you worked every day.

Today's flexible corporation nurtures a different ethos. The premium is on manipulating others through superficial cooperation and flexibility. These dynamics put workers right in touch with the narcissist lifestyle. Likewise, the insincere people skills required by the team captain and the worker who deals with clients are driven by the desire to accumulate admirers that typifies narcissism.

There is at least one other dynamic associated with the prevailing business-management technique that fosters a narcissist ethos. With the team concept, excellence in work is harder to judge than when individual accountability for a specific assignment is the model. Consequently, promotions and dismissals tend not to be based on clear, fixed rules, with crisply defined tasks. How one relates to networks has become the determining factor in determining one's professional success.[44] The lack of clarity about these standards for success makes for more anxiety in today's workplace than in the old system, where you knew more or less where you stood on the basis of productivity levels.

In such an ethos, the need for approval has become more important than one's accomplishments. The late Christopher Lasch described these dynamics well:

> In a society in which the dream of success has been drained of any meaning beyond itself, men have nothing against which to measure their achievements except the achievements of others. Self-approval depends on public recognition. . . . Today men seek the kind of approval that applauds not their actions but their personal attributes. They wish to be not so much esteemed

as admired. They crave not fame but the glamour and excitement of celebrity. They want to be envied rather than respected.[45]

Anyone who has been involved in the daily life of a large American institution or a professional guild knows that this is the way success is measured in new-millennium America, the way that power is exercised (or flaunted). Narcissism is good for the new economy.

We should not fail to remind ourselves about points made in the introduction concerning how the rampant consumerism related to the outbreak of narcissism in America has aided the new economy with respect to more than the workforce. Narcissists are also potentially great consumers. The narcissist is never satisfied, always seeking to be titillated with novelty and the latest fashion. Such a consumer is precisely what the new economy needs. Awareness that a narcissist consumer will not be loyal to the products recently bought feeds modern business's drive for flexibility in the products it sells. And because the narcissist personality is so good for business, it is no accident that the media, controlled as it is by business interests, have another vested interest in extolling and nurturing the narcissist lifestyle.

No two ways about it. Some narcissism is good for contemporary business. But such personality traits and the optimistic view of human nature that have made them possible are not so good for our common well-being.

Conclusion: Augustinian Economic Common Sense

An appreciation of the Augustinian view of human nature is an important insight for dealing with the economic realities of the new millennium. When we approach contemporary business realities with an Augustinian worldview, we become a little cynical about what is happening. In fact, the relative silencing of this worldview allowed for the naïveté about business practices and the relaxation of government surveillance that made possible the Enron and WorldCom scandals. The Augustinian worldview helps Americans more readily see the oppressive character of modern business and the dangers of its monopoly on American life. Such a worldview can help us to recognize how the system is rigged in favor of the wealthy and the entrepreneur. Yet an Augustinian vision also teaches tolerance, for a deep understanding of the way in which concupiscence makes the system work reminds us that we would do the same thing as the bosses were we in their position, and that they are as vulnerable to the dynamics as we are.

America needs a revival of this Augustinian worldview for other reasons. It was earlier noted that the inequality of the new economy is further rigged against the majority by the ideology that those in charge have developed—the ideology of the "meritocracy." Read the work of Clinton's first secretary of labor, Robert Reich, for an articulate promulgation of this ideology.[46] Certainly, the image of his former boss as one of the "brightest and the best" to rise from humble beginnings fostered this ideology. In fact, his embodiment of this image may help explain the Clinton mystique and account for his support by so many whose career trajectories seemed like his (or those who at least had married men with similar trajectories or with aspirations to such trajectories—the so-called "soccer moms").

The idea of a meritocracy clearly presupposes the optimistic Enlightenment viewpoint that all human beings have an equal chance, that opportunity is equally accessible to all. Of course, what gets missed in such an optimistic ideology are things like accidents of birth (specifically genetic gifts of intelligence) and the "luck" of getting into one of the status schools. If you did not get that advantageous head start, you will probably not "merit" a life of success. But those data are not ideologically admissible (no one acknowledges them) in our present social climate. It takes Augustinian realism to believe them.

Without a revival of an Augustinian/constitutional perspective on human nature, it is unlikely that we are going to begin seriously to challenge the present dominance of business in our culture at the expense of labor. As a result of these dynamics, it is little wonder that quality of life is increasingly diminished in our time. Little wonder that America continues to slip in this area, falling behind Western European nations, notably Norway and Sweden.[47] It is increasingly evident how much we need a popularized Augustinian view of human nature to aid the American worker by awakening the public to the fact that given our concupiscent nature, adversarial relationships between employee and employer are inevitable. The relationship will never be a just one as long as the power rests unevenly with management, as it does currently. Recovering a sense of original sin can drive us to an awareness that only when labor/management tensions are public and subject to governance by fair rules will economics be (relatively) fair. Until that happens, expect the rich to get richer, the poor to get poorer, and the middle class to shrink. Do not be surprised if we also become increasingly narcissistic in our public ethos and a little more unhappy.

five

Religion and the Real World

An Entertaining Religious Life without Sin and Guilt

Large segments of American religion (especially the so-called mainline Protestant denominations) have been caught up by the craze for business and its new management techniques, therapy, instant gratification, and even German Enlightenment optimism. It will quickly become evident that at least for American Christian communities, a strong dose of Augustine is badly needed.

Although the child abuse scandals that rocked the Catholic Church had the immediate effect of causing a decline in Americans' confidence in religion, throughout much of the 1990s religious organizations held the highest levels of confidence from the American public among all major institutions. Over 60 percent of Americans expressed a "great deal" or "quite a lot" of confidence in them. Higher education comes close, and public schools are not too bad (though far lower in the category of those expressing a great deal of confidence). The media and the federal government, as previously noted, garnered only 28.3 percent and 23.7 percent, respectively. This figure is down since 1975–1985, when it scored in the 60s.[1]

Clergy were among the highest ranked of trusted occupational groups in America according to a late 1997 Gallup poll, with 17 percent of the public ranking them very high in trust-

119

worthiness. However, when we lump together those who rate very high and high in the esteem of the public, pharmacists actually commanded higher percentages (69 percent, as compared to 59 percent for the clergy).[2]

Certainly, being a pastor or a priest in mainline Christian circles does not have the prestige it once did. For reasons probably related to the unique history of American Judaism, this dynamic does not seem to typify modern Judaism. In any case, Christian pastors are regularly hassled by parishioners, and the number of pastors in mainline Protestant denominations forced out by their congregations has grown dramatically in the last thirty years. For example, in the nation's largest Protestant denomination, the Southern Baptist Convention, over 760 pastors were reportedly fired in 2000. The erosion of authority associated with narcissism and the celebrity culture are having their impact on American religion. Also, the high expectations of human nature, which an optimistic Enlightenment view of human nature imposes on its adherents, entails that they are more likely to be disappointed with the flaws of their leaders than they would be had they an Augustinian outlook on the fallibility of human nature.

In August 1997, 62 percent of the American public (80 percent of Black respondents and 59 percent of the Whites) claimed religion was very important for them—up from 1990, but down from 1953, when 75 percent of the public made that claim. Not much had changed by the time of a 2000–2001 survey by the Barna Research Group, as 68 percent of its adult respondents claimed that religion was important for them.[3] Eighty-six percent of the public claimed to believe in God, but not necessarily in a conventional way.[4] Six in ten Americans claimed to read the Bible at least occasionally (though such polls usually reveal some statistical exaggeration of the reality, since subjects would typically rather appear religious to the pollsters).[5] In a 2001 poll of the Barna Research Group, 82 percent of Americans reported that they prayed regularly and 24 percent claimed to have shared their faith with a nonbeliever in the previous year.

It is interesting in this connection to note that although there was an immediate surge in American religiosity immediately following the catastrophic events of September 11, 2001, the Barna Research Group has shown that within two months of the attacks "virtually every spiritual indicator available suggested that things were back to pre-attack levels."[6] This might come as a shock to those who believed that life had dramatically changed in America after the attacks. But for those chastened by an Augustinian and constitutional cynicism about how American attitudes typically are modified by the latest wind of change, this is no surprise.

Customizing Religious Belief

There is a definite (unfocused) spiritual sensibility among the broader American public. At least as recently as 1996, 72 percent of the public believed in angels, 56 percent in the devil, and 48 percent in ESP. A more recent survey indicated that nearly seven in ten American adults believed in a God who is an all-powerful creator. In fact, nearly half of Americans reject the theory of evolution in favor of a biblical belief in the creation of humanity in its present form by God.[7] This eclectic sort of religious commitment is evident in that nearly 40 percent of the American public claimed that there is much in their religion that they do not believe.[8]

This is not to say that religious communities have been completely abandoned. As recently as August 1997, a Gallup poll reported that 68 percent of Americans claimed to be members of either a synagogue or a church, that 29 percent attended weekly and 12 percent almost weekly.[9] (Again, though, we must keep in mind the gap between what Americans tell pollsters about what they do and their actual religious practice.)

These data and the observations of various social analysts confirm what those engaged in religious work have recognized for some time. Except perhaps among recent immigrant families, religion has become almost totally a matter of choice, no longer a matter of ethnicity or loyalty to the way one was raised. This is in marked contrast to 1955, when a Gallup poll showed that only one American in twenty-five no longer adhered to the faith of his or her childhood. Today it is the majority, if not nearly all Americans, who have this experience.[10] With these dynamics, many begin to regard religion and its truths as subjective.[11]

These dynamics reflect the degree to which our narcissist social trends have even permeated American religious dynamics. Like every other reality, religion has begun to lose its own objective character to function primarily as an object to serve needs.

Another compatible way of assessing these dynamics is to recognize that in placing oneself above the truths of religion, in reducing it to a meeting of one's needs, the presupposition is that people are good. They know what they need, and their instincts about the truth are accurate and good. Only sinners need the binding authority of the religious community's authoritative teachings to get them on the right path. The good person already has a vision of the right way to go. Select religious teachings are merely a vehicle for supplementing generally sound life instincts.

But once religion is personalized in this way, as it seems to be in America, once what I believe and the community I belong to is a matter of choice relevant insofar as it meets my needs, then ecclesiastical institutions like the church become less and less important.[12] As a number of analysts have noted, this trend is becoming especially evident among the Generation Xers. One of these analysts, Tom Beaudoin, puts the matter this way:

> "If you want to talk about the church, I'm not very interested." That was perhaps the single most common sentence that I heard from Xers over the past several years in discussions and interviews. Most frequently, this statement was followed with something like, "I still think people can be spiritual or religious without going to churches and synagogues." Some even added the rhetorical question, "Do you think it really makes a difference to God?"[13]

Of particular interest in connection with the anti-ecclesiastic orientation of the Xers is a study made by Beaudoin of the music videos marketed to them. Many of these videos attack the church for domesticating Jesus. A good example is the work of Madonna and her redefinition of religious icons like the crucifix.[14] We have here, then, another example of how the public has been manipulated by the values portrayed in the media. Little wonder that negative feelings toward religious organizations would begin to surface in public opinion, given the media's bias against organized religion. Of course, the youngest generation most prone to influence by the media (the Xers) is most persuaded by its messages.

There were indications over a decade ago that a broad social consensus regarding the irrelevance of religious institutions was beginning to form. A poll of Christians taken by the Barna Research Group revealed that only 28 percent of adult Christians strongly agreed that "the Christian churches in your area are relevant to the way you live today."[15] These are serious problems that lie ahead, for according to the polls those who have the most use for the church are the elderly or those in their fifties, who when they die are not likely to be replaced in the church by Generation Xers. In fact, Barna more recently concluded that "compared to teens throughout the past 20 years, today's teenagers have the lowest likelihood of attending church when they are living independently of their parents."[16]

That denominations (especially those of the Protestant mainline) are in decline is well known. The membership decline since the 1960s has been highlighted. There has been a steady decline—more than a 20 percent loss since 1980—in the Christian Church (Disciples of Christ), the Episcopal Church, and the United Church of Christ, as well as a double-figure percentage loss in the United Methodist Church. More recently, the Barna Group has also documented declines in financial stewardship in terms of the percentage of Americans who made contributions in 2000 as compared to previous years. Even born-again Christians gave less money on the average.[17]

Another sphere in which American religion is not doing well pertains to its general lack of impact on public issues. Noted Yale Law School professor Stephen Carter has made this case eloquently. Essentially, Carter laments that in educated and public policy circles views articulated by religious leaders are deemed sectarian, not relevant to the common good. Granted, he concedes, it is appropriate to utter platitudes about God blessing America or about the grace of God. But these are not distinctively Jewish, Muslim, or Christian insights. They are merely the rhetoric of American civil religion (a set of affirmations that claim divine sanction for the nation's or one's favorite policies). However, as soon as one moves to theological arguments that are distinctly Christian, Jewish, etc., the appropriateness of one's rhetoric begins to come into question. Fanaticism is likely to be the media's charge.[18] One thinks of the media's and the general public's reactions to the Religious Right and the religiosity of Jimmy Carter and Joe Lieberman. (If you want to experience intolerance of these perspectives, spend some time in the academy at a faculty gathering or a professional society meeting.) As Stephen Carter puts it, "God is alright as long as it is just a hobby."[19]

Recent poll results from the Barna Research Group seem to lend further credence to this intuition about the irrelevance of religious commitments. Polling conducted in May 2001 showed that only one in four American adults leaned primarily on religious principles when making moral decisions, while 44 percent cited that their prime norm was to do whatever would bring about the most pleasing results (along with another 17 percent who based moral decisions on what they believed would make people happy or minimize conflict).[20]

We need to examine how this disinterest in institutional religion developed and what the church can do about it. With regard to the latter, the standard answer of late has been to point to the techniques espoused by the Church Growth Movement (its advocacy of professional marketing techniques, targeting one's audience, and offering entertaining worship) and to note the phenomenal growth of so-called megachurches, many of which adopted these church growth techniques and seem to have grown because of them. Many of these megachurches are also characterized by a "seeker spirituality," targeting the experience of Baby Boomers and Generation Xers who seek to find meaning in the numbing bustle (and, for the

Xers, in the midst of their sense of the betrayals) of their daily life. However, some analysts believe that the day of the megachurch and its seeker spirituality may be beginning to ebb, that there will be a desire to return to the moderate-size church, where there is some sense of the community of the whole without totally forgoing the virtues of a programmatic church.[21]

Though important differences exist, the underlying experiential focus of the spirituality of the megachurches bears affinities to the theology that has dominated the academy since the Enlightenment, itself rooted in an experiential starting point.[22] (The difference may be that seeker-church spirituality has found a way to depict experience more in touch with the cultural idiom and in more creative ways than the prevailing models of the academy.) But as we shall note, this prevailing theology is to a great extent the premier culprit in accounting for the progressive decline of the social impact of American Christianity; it seems that the theology of the seeker may not be the way back from the wilderness for the church.

These comments also help introduce reflections on how lack of interest in American institutional religion has come to pass. It has to do with the character of the prevailing models of religious thought since the Enlightenment and their inability to withstand the onslaughts of all the sociocultural dynamics of the nineteenth, twentieth, and twenty-first centuries. The situation has been all the more exacerbated since the 1970s, because it has been only since that decade that the prevailing academic theological model truly became embedded in the American pew.

The Psychologizing of American Religion: It's Got to Be Reasonable, Soothing, and Entertaining

Just as the therapeutic paradigm (looking at realities in light of psychological insights) has come to dominate in many areas of American life, it is hardly surprising that psychological jargon and ways of functioning have become dominant in much of the American religious community (particularly but not exclusively in the largest mainline Protestant denominations). But to understand how that happened we need to review briefly the history of Christian theology since the Enlightenment.

It is commonly maintained that the nineteenth-century German Evangelical theologian Friedrich Schleiermacher was the father of modern Christian theology.[23] Essentially, Schleiermacher broke with the prevailing orthodox Protestant models of theology, which initiated theological reflection from the perspective of an inerrant Bible, and instead undertook an apology for Christianity by trying to relate it to the credible worldview of his day (i.e., romantic philosophy).[24] The majority of Christian theologians since his time have sought to do the same, albeit with a different worldview as the framework in which the concepts of Christian faith were to be interpreted. The agenda was to seek to make faith reasonable by showing that it speaks to contemporary experience.

Schleiermacher's thought did not just open the door to the translation of Christian faith into the categories of psychology. (Of course, this was a natural development in that if one elects not to employ the categories of romanticism, which Schleiermacher did for rendering Christianity relevant to the modern mind, any other conceptual category of the day will do. It does not matter if it is existential philosophy, feminist theory, Marxism, or psychology.) His thought also brought into the church's pulpits and Sunday schools a tacit acknowledgment of a number of the Enlightenment's intellectual commitments, notably its critical perspective on religious authority and its optimistic view of human nature.

Schleiermacher's thought evolved in a context in which critical assessments of the truth and authority of the Bible were being developed (an approach to biblical studies called historical criticism). The whole concept of the sort of apologetics in which he engaged presupposes that biblical concepts can no longer be taken literally but must be reinterpreted in light of contemporary experience. Thus, to engage in a theology like Schleiermacher's is to some extent to concede that the Bible and the classical Christian tradition are not fruitfully read literally, that truth lies deeper than in the historicity or scientific veracity of the claims Scripture seems to make. Again, the goal of this approach, of showing how reasonable faith is, how it does not demand intellectual assent to ideas hard for the modern mind to accept, is also evident in this set of commitments.

Naturally, in an increasingly secular society, Christians have been encountering these suppositions for several centuries. But the widespread adoption of Schleiermacher's model of theology has brought the suppositions into the church, as recent polls indicate. A poll completed in June 2001 by the Barna Research Group revealed that only 26 percent of American Catholics and only 34 percent of mainline Protestants believed that the Bible is totally accurate.[25]

Enlightenment optimism is implied in Schleiermacher's theology and in that of all contemporaries who use his method, insofar as there is a supposition that modern people have got things right about their self-understanding. If my task as a theologian is to interpret my religious tradition into the categories of modern experience, the presupposition is that I am not so warped as to misunderstand my situation. I am asking the right questions. In a sense I am on the right track.

Given these suppositions, sin becomes primarily a failure to achieve what we need. The Christian life is then construed as a way to meet those needs. Heirs of Schleiermacher's theology can thus disengage original sin from concupiscence and selfishness, because living holy lives is about meeting our needs.[26] It is a short step, then, to reduce sin to unhealthy behaviors that do not meet needs and to contend likewise that in "healthy" behavior we overcome sin.

Of course this optimism about the self embedded in Schleiermacher's theology accords with the way most modern people think about themselves, and the task of theology on grounds of his model is to relate faith to modern suppositions. Recall the 2000 *New York Times* poll noted in the introduction that revealed that 73 percent of Americans claimed that people are good and that 85 percent thought they could be pretty much anything they wanted to be. Given the impact of Schleiermacher's theological suppositions and their implicit endorsement of such modern thinking, it is not surprising that these very un-Augustinian, unconstitutional views of human nature have permeated the American pews. We can see the dynamics involved in these developments more clearly in light of the psychologizing of American religion.

By no means was the liberal theology of Schleiermacher an instant success in America. Approaches like his had their adherents in America in his own lifetime, but they tended to be located in the elite Protestant theological institutions (though as the nineteenth century turned into the twentieth, some adherents were occupying prestigious pulpits and the headquarters of the most Americanized denominations). In large part the fundamentalist movement of the first decades of the twentieth century was a reaction against these developments. It was only after World War II that this approach and the widespread endorsement of historical-critical approaches to the study of the Bible began to gain general acceptance in most American theological seminaries. (Since the Second Vatican Council in the 1960s, even Catholics can legitimately endorse these agendas.[27])

The result has been that, more and more, this has become the theology of the ordinary town pulpit, and the media have more effectively engendered their discrediting of traditional Judeo-Christian beliefs, and so large numbers of Americans have been raised in churches that have taught them a piety reflecting Schleiermachian suppositions. We have already seen this with regard to American Christian attitudes toward biblical authority. In addition, there are other ways in which such an impact is obvious.

The establishment of the study of pastoral care, presented by instructors in therapeutic categories, as a requirement in most American seminaries, and a "professionalizing" dynamic that demands that most candidates for ordination present themselves as psychologically healthy individuals, have been real turning points in the psychologizing of American religion. With Schleiermacher (and, more influentially in America, an adherent of his approach, Paul Tillich) exerting increased influence on academic thinking about religion, the obvious step was the use of psychological categories, rather than those of romantic or existential philosophy, as the framework into which traditional Christian concepts were interpreted. And with good old American pragmatism having its influence even within the religious fold, it has become almost a creed in most mainline churches that this sort of translating of classical beliefs into psychological categories is the most "practical" way to do ministry. Seminary students buy into this assumption, and so bring the Schleiermachian model with them into the parishes they serve, on the grounds that it is more practical and people-centered.

To practice Christian ministry is to be engaged in therapy. As one early proponent of this vision wrote:

> Society as a whole needs patterns of community life which will help ordinary people to fulfill themselves in much the same sort of way that psychiatrists help those who are specially troubled. Building up such community life would surely be a directly Christian activity. . . . [Churchpeople can become such professional therapists] only if they break way from almost all, if not all, of their traditional religious pursuits.[28]

In essence, the gospel that is now preached in churches with this sort of leadership is a gospel of self-fulfillment. This trend was noted as early as the mid-1960s by the eminent cultural analyst Philip Rieff. As he put it: "Any religious activity is justified only by being something men do for themselves, that is, for the enrichment of their own experience."[29]

As therapy involves enhancement of the self, so religion is now interpreted by more and more Americans as an exercise in enhancing self-fulfillment. This is hardly surprising, for as several analysts have noted, psychology directs clients to focus more on obligations to oneself than to others.[30] The impact of these suppositions on much of American religious thought and on the attitudes of many of the faithful is both evident and disconcerting.

The therapeutic model and the gospel of self-fulfillment are evident in a number of ways in American religious life. Congregations are expected to "entertain," to meet parishioners' needs. One early statement of this philosophy of church growth envisaged a church that

> . . . will be a place for the celebration of life, and its characteristics will be spontaneity and acceptance. . . . It will be a place of colour, movement, and vitality where young and old will not only look at what men of past ages have painted, listen to what they have written and the music they have made, but where they themselves will be free to paint, dance, talk, and express themselves in ways no longer easy in an age of automation, nonemployment, space sickness, and leisure lostness. Few, if any places in the new society will offer such arresting and beckoning horizons of human creativity.[31]

Of course, in certain respects the gospel does soothe and is entertaining, but those are by-products of the forgiving love of God. When these emotional responses become ends in themselves, the piety produced is preoccupied with self-seeking (as believers praise God only to get something out of it for themselves). It is task-oriented (worship leaders and worshipers feel pressure to perform in a certain way to achieve entertaining and soothing effects) and ephemeral (as what entertains and soothes does not last forever). The Christian fed by this style of spirituality is very much alone, isolated from the church's heritage, and isolated from contemporaries and the present experience of God, precisely because so much of the focus is on finding *self* (-fulfillment and -affirmation).

A religious worldview influenced by this model of spirituality is so preoccupied with finding the self and being affirmed that its prophetic voice becomes ineffectual. We can see this in the way in which many of the mainline Protestant churches have bought into some of the "political correctness" ideology of the media and of the intellectual establishment that shall be subsequently described. For it is simply "bad manners" in these circles today to raise questions about practices that were

not long ago unequivocally condemned in these same denominations, about such topics as the ordination of practicing
homosexuals, women's ordination, remarriage after divorce,
and, increasingly, even premarital sex. (It is interesting to note
that most of these commitments are still affirmed by the Religious Right, which in turn entails that the Religious Right
tends to function as a kind of politically incorrect whipping
boy in much of mainstream American religion.) So much in
touch with the attitudes of many American opinion makers
and with public consensus are these commitments that the
mainstream religious community has become a handmaid of
the culture; it has lost the countercultural perspective that religion at its best displays.

We can also observe these dynamics in the increased unwillingness of religious bodies in America to take radical socially
ethical positions that regard the structures of government as
fallen and requiring reform. Most Christian social action in our
era has taken the form of pronouncements on personal morality (especially condemning homosexuality and advocating cut-
backs in welfare to "get the chiselers") or in defense of spiritual expression in the schools. The implicit assumption of such
preoccupation with individual morality is that human beings
are essentially good and will correct their moral lapses. In these
respects too, American religion seems to be just echoing what
the majority of Americans today believe.

Another, previously mentioned, manifestation of the loss of
the prophetic voice is that it has become increasingly difficult
at the local level to condemn sin. Christian preachers consistently report that they receive negative feedback from parishioners if they address the topic, even if just in a pedagogical
way. "We came here to feel good, not to be run down" is the
new litany of many American churchgoers. If sin is to be mentioned at all without controversy, it can only be portrayed as
nothing more than mistaken or unhealthy behaviors and outlooks that impede our happiness.

Given the optimism about human nature revealed in the previously noted *New York Times* poll, it is perhaps not surprising
that such negative reactions to the condemnation of sin would

emerge. But it is a bit startling to see the data regarding how thoroughly acculturated in Protestant churches this optimism has become. As recently as 1991, a poll by the Barna Research Group revealed that 77 percent of American Christians (almost 90 percent of mainline Protestants) believed that people were basically good, a figure that was not much lower than the figure for non-Christians.[32]

Such a forfeiture of belief in the doctrine of original sin is not the only indication of how American religion is being distorted by its co-optation by the therapeutic paradigm. Other manifestations of how the psychologizing of American religion has led to the development of a spirituality preoccupied with finding the self and being affirmed are painfully evident. Here too in a Christian context they testify to the distortion of faith.

One such example is how Jesus' directive to "love your neighbor as yourself" (Mark 12:31) is regularly interpreted in the pews. In the best traditions of therapy and narcissism, more and more mainline Protestants have come to believe that Jesus wants us to learn to love ourselves (as if concupiscent people did not spend most of their time trying to do that). The next assertion is that we cannot love others until we love ourselves.[33] It sounds like selfish *eros* love, not the self-emptying *agape* love that Jesus exhorts and embodies. But then love as self-sacrifice or submission to a higher loyalty is regarded as injurious to personal health from a therapeutic point of view, and it is the latter set of values that dominates the cultural and ecclesiastical air in America today.[34] What once counted as sin (selfishness) in the traditions of Christian faith is now construed as redemptive.

The theological approach of Schleiermacher and his heirs, which undergirds this psychologizing of America, also opens the way to redefinitions of God. No less an august source than the *Wall Street Journal* recently noted that Americans have come regularly to redefine God to suit their own tastes. Thus God is Black for some African-American theologians and a woman for some feminists.[35] When we psychologize our religion, we make religion a vehicle for our own needs.

These redefinitions of God to suit our own needs are also related to the new styles in worship that have become typical throughout the most "Americanized" segments of the church in the United States. Informal worship styles are what the church growth experts advocate, and the success of such worship styles in building some megachurches seems to bear out the wisdom of this advice. Especially since the 1970s, the dress code is down in most American churches. Most Baby Boomers and younger generations no longer wear coat and tie to church, and slacks are in for women. Relaxed informality is the name of the game.

When informality is in, awe and mystery are lost. That has been the end result of these trends. A god who is no longer awesome is a god we can manipulate and redefine to suit our aims. This new portrayal of God is related to the loss of the sense of unworthiness (the diminution of the sense of sin) that we have observed in much Protestantism and in American society as a whole. The good person is more comfortable in the presence of God, more likely to take God for granted. It is only the sinner who is likely to "tremble . . . tremble . . . tremble."

There is another, no less serious, distortion of the faith that has resulted from the diminution of original sin coupled with these propensities to make God in our own image. The theological seminaries of Western Christianity have unwittingly contributed to this, not just by the widespread endorsement of the Schleiermachian model of theology and the pastoral care appropriations of this model, which systematically psychologize the content of Christian faith. The biblical roots of the doctrine of original sin have been under fire since the invention of historical-critical approaches to the study of the Bible in the nineteenth century. In consequence of a highly influential 1961 article entitled "The Apostle Paul and the Introspective Conscience of the West" by the eminent Swedish New Testament scholar Krister Stendahl, the majority of New Testament courses have challenged the Augustinian reading of Paul as teaching that God's law always condemns sin.[36] Rather, it is maintained, guilt over sin is not at all Paul's agenda.

(It is interesting to note that Stendahl's article was originally written for and so probably reflects the influence of an audience of therapists.)

The result of generations of propounding these intellectual trends and associated commitments in the pews is that American Christians have come to see religion as something for which they must take responsibility. A recently completed poll of the Barna Research Group revealed the striking fact that only 27 percent of mainline Protestants and 9 percent of Catholics, and only 30 percent of all Americans surveyed, believed that we are not saved by works.[37] These striking data entail that the vast majority of Americans hold a faith that is no longer recognizably in touch with the core of the Reformation or with church teachings since the time of Augustine.

In its present state the majority, though not all of American Christianity, is in no position to function as a counter-voice to the trends in American society we have been noting. (The poll indicated that there was a bit more of an awareness of the historic Christian position on salvation by grace among members of theologically conservative churches associated with the Evangelical movement. More on that later.) American religion in all its forms, even Christianity, is now little more than an echo of American society's preoccupation with doing for yourself and making it on your own, because we are fundamentally good people. It has even bought into the latest business paradigms.

Business Has Become the Church's Business

The Schleiermachian model for theology has been employed by some church leaders not so much to relate faith commitments to the therapeutic outlook as to authorize reliance on more efficient modes of administration. With the rise of our present business ethos, religious communities have felt pressure to function more efficiently. The result has been the uncritical adoption of the latest business-management techniques by these communities, notably, but not exclusively, at the denominational level. As in the case of the psychologizing of American religion, here too examples abound.

Thus it is no accident that the majority of continuing education events for mainline Protestant clergy focus on more efficient congregational management or on the development of computer skills or counseling skills, and only occasionally get around to biblical studies and theology. Business techniques are more and more evident in today's ecclesiastical fund-raising activities. For generations, only the Catholic Church relied on gambling to raise funds. In recent decades, even denominations long opposed to fund-raisers regularly sell beverages, have their youth do car washes, or charge fees for congregational meals in order to supplement their budgets. Whatever happened to the church's mandate to witness to *agape* love, which is to be given away freely without any benefit to the self?

Another typical example of the inroads of contemporary management techniques is evident in the widely accepted reinterpretation of the New Testament concept of the priesthood of all believers (1 Peter 2:9; Rev. 20:6) as an authorization for a critique of the exercise of pastoral authority in favor of more lay autonomy in decision making. No less characteristic has been the propensity of religious bodies to draw their lay leadership almost exclusively from professional and other elite classes. The reason for these choices, it is insisted, is that these persons are the most highly qualified, the best people available. Never mind that these are lay people whose values are more in line with the business and therapeutic culture endorsed by the religious leaders themselves, and not so much of the average working-class member of the religious body.

This sort of personnel and appointment system is likely to minimize conflict and make the "team" (committee or governing body) to which the laity have been appointed run more smoothly. Pastors are trained in professional schools, are accustomed to manipulating information, and know the therapeutic ethos, and at least the denominational bureaucrats and megachurch pastors even have some commitment to the latest management techniques. Lay people with similar backgrounds are their natural allies in the denomination, as they will speak the same language. Little wonder that it is they who serve on governing-body committees and boards.

My own Evangelical Lutheran Church in America illustrates this pattern well. During its creation through merger in the mid-1980s, a committee was appointed to facilitate the process. Of the thirty-eight lay members, twenty-five held jobs associated with the class of managers and professionals. Although warnings were issued about this imbalance, and some of the bishops of one of the predecessor bodies of the merged denomination expressed concern about true inclusiveness, the lessons were not learned. In 1989 there was much controversy about the composition of a task force on human sexuality for the new denomination, controversy about whether it was efficient to add a conservative. Only subsequently was one added, one who was "reasonable."[38]

A similar bias toward placing professionals (business executives and educators) in the highest lay positions in mainline denominations is evident in the United Methodist Church. At its 2000 General Conference (the denomination's highest governing authority), of those lay delegates not retired, the vast majority held such jobs. The Executive Council of the United Church of Christ seems to have a similar job profile among a significant majority of its lay members. Even the Executive Committee of the Southern Baptist Convention draws only 10 percent to 12 percent of its eighty-one lay members from the ranks of blue-collar workers.

In view of the unrepresentative character of those who frame them, it is hardly surprising that denominational activities are so irrelevant to so many American congregations and the people who occupy the pews. The decline in denominational loyalty and the individualism associated with the psychologizing of American religion are factors. But the bias of these religious bodies toward the values of society's elite, and their estrangement from the masses of their members as a result of their adoption of the latest management suppositions, are undeniable. Just as in business the uncritical reliance on the team model overlooks an Augustinian vision that would remind us how easy it is to exploit those not in power, so American religion in its mainline expressions is losing its ability to represent those removed from power, because it has uncritically embraced the latest management techniques.

The Augustinian Corrective

The sort of bleak portrait I have been painting of American religion is not the whole story. It is interesting to consider that the fastest-growing American religious bodies tend to be theologically conservative. These are churches that have not bought into the Schleiermachian paradigm and its associated psychologizing of religion or uncritical endorsement of the latest management techniques.

For example, since 1980, while mainline denominations have declined in membership, theologically conservative churches have grown. The Evangelical Free Church of America grew by a phenomenal 210.7 percent, the International Church of the Foursquare Gospel by 139.2 percent, the Church of God (Cleveland, Tennessee) by 100 percent, and the Assemblies of God by 48.6 percent. The theologically conservative African-American Pentecostal Church of God in Christ soared by 48.3 percent until 1991 (the most recent year reported), while a number of the other historic, but more mainline Black denominations, like the African Methodist Episcopal Zion Church and the Christian Methodist Episcopal Church, held their own and even grew slightly in this era of general membership losses. The Roman Catholic Church, which in many parishes continues to retain certain ethnic ties to the "old country," also has grown significantly since Word War II, as its share of the U.S. population has risen 1 percent to 1.5 percent per decade.

This reality provides a formula for reviving American religion, one that is Augustinian just as my prescription is for our sociopolitical realities. Survey data from the Barna Research Group revealed that theologically conservative churches have succeeded in preserving belief in the accuracy of the Bible, in Christ's sinlessness, and in the doctrine that works do not earn heaven far better than has the American public as a whole (between 66 percent and 81 percent, in comparison to 34 percent for mainline Protestants regarding biblical authority; between 55 percent and 73 percent in comparison to 33 percent for mainline Protestants, regarding Christ's sinlessness; and between 43 percent and 64 percent in comparison to 30 percent for mainline Protestants regarding the rejection of works as a basis for salvation).[39] It is evident that the theological conservatism of these churches has allowed their members to retain the Augustinian insight about the fallenness of humanity (our inability to earn salvation) in a way that more theologically liberal churches have not. These are churches that have a better chance to be able to call America back to its Augustinian-constitutional roots.

The recently completed survey of American congregations called "Faith Communities in the United States Today" also provides data that explain why historic African-American churches and other religious groups with some ethnic roots have not experienced as much membership attrition as have mainline Protestant bodies. (The sole exception of a religious body with strong ethnic ties that is losing members is Judaism, which has lost nearly half its members in the decades since World War II.) It seems that in an age of apparently declining denominational loyalty, African-American congregations have the highest appreciation of denominational heritage (74 percent), followed by Latino congregations and White congregations (both Protestant and Catholic) with ethnic roots (tied at 69 percent).[40] With such denominational loyalty we can assume some cognizance of and loyalty to the teachings of the denominations of those members. Thus these congregations are likely to reflect more of an appreciation of classical Christian affirmations like the Augustinian view of original sin than are those Christian groups with a lower denominational consciousness. The conservatism associated with an ethnic consciousness is apparently good for preserving theological orthodoxy.

Preservation of theological orthodoxy is obviously good for church growth, as the statistics show. It is also good for vibrancy of congregational life, as the same survey of American congregations showed that congregations high on denominational heritage are more likely to have financial health than those that do not have such denominational loyalty.[41]

It is evident that the most vibrant religious faith appears to develop when the religious bodies in question are countercultural, breaking with the basic suppositions of the German Enlightenment. Of course, there is a genuine sense in which Christian bodies that fall into this category are very much in touch with core American values (especially the Constitution's Augustinianism). As such, it is in the interests of all segments of the American church to seek to recover the Augustinian view of human persons. It could serve not only to render them more spiritually healthy but also to make them a more effective voice in contemporary American society.

This strategy offers a promising way to break the impasse in the school prayer debate as well as that in the debate over religion in the schools. A church that is calling attention to the roots of the Constitution in Augustinian thought and points out how America's founders' appeal to the natural law as a basis for government is compatible with the biblical witness (see the Declaration of Independence's appeal to the "Laws of Nature"; cf. Romans 2:14–15) effectively makes the case for the Christian roots of the American system (in a way that does not exclude other religious commitments). An American church confidently articulating these themes and nurturing scholars and public opinion committed to these insights will eventually get them into the curriculum of American public education, and in so doing help stem the tide of present constitutional ignorance and the feel-good optimism of our present narcissist social ethos.

six

Sex, Marriage, and Family without Common Sense

The revolutions transpiring in the so-called "private sphere" of American society since the 1960s have largely been driven by our adoption of the optimistic views of German Enlightenment conceptions of human nature, especially the therapeutic view of reality. As a result, a lot of narcissist thinking permeates contemporary American views of sex, marriage, and family.

As we have observed, the priority in all human relationships is now conceived in terms of flexibility and fulfillment of the self. Consequently, relationships to family are not understood as binding, as shaping of and prior to the self's gratification. To go back to the old style would be to retreat to "unhealthy" behaviors, since essentially good human beings can never be totally wrong when they follow their current desires. This dynamic and its correlated ideology about human nature help explain the increase in divorce, the much-lamented alleged neglect of our children, and the so-called sexual revolution.

A little Augustinian realism and appreciation of the essential selfishness of human nature can go a long way toward stabilizing the institution of marriage. It could teach the public not to expect too much from marriage. As a result, we might not be so insistent on thinking of marriage as an institution intended primarily for meeting our own needs, and so be more inclined to stick it out in hard times. Likewise, Augustinianism reminds us that good as they are, sex and parenting have their risks and responsibilities. More on those points later. For the present, it is important to assess the monumental changes in the private sphere that have exacerbated the revolutions under way.

The New Realities Regarding Sexual Behavior

A 2001 Gallup poll, completed just prior to the economic downturn of the immediate post-Clinton years, revealed that concerns about family, ethics, and morality were perceived alongside education as one of the most important problems for the country. Even when their pocketbooks became less insecure, Americans still worried a lot about family decline.[1]

The significant changes in the American way of life and the negative effects of some of these changes have gotten the public's attention. The number of women in the labor force has taken a notable jump, from 31.3 million in 1970 to 71.8 million in 1999. The number of working women with children from ages six to seventeen nearly doubled, increasing from 7.6 million in 1970 to 15.1 million in 1999. The number of working women with children under the age of six more than doubled, rising from 4.5 million to 10.3 million![2]

In a sense this phenomenon has effectively contributed to the gap between rich and poor, because when combined with the feminist movement and the increased numbers of professional women with college degrees, a new phenomenon in marriage has transpired. Highly educated professional men are marrying women with similar backgrounds. The female secretary or nurse no longer marries the boss or the doctor. Instead, she marries the guy with a blue-collar job, and the professional man marries another executive, doctor, or lawyer. This has marked implications for the wealth that two-income professional families are accumulating relative to those with jobs at the lower end of the salary scale.[3]

We noted earlier the sevenfold increase in the number of cohabiting heterosexual couples since 1990 and the fivefold increase in the number of divorces since 1950. The previously observed marked increase in the public's recognition of the acceptability of "shacking up" (54 percent of mainline Protestants) is also no doubt related to data discerned in a 1996 Gallup poll. It found that 31 percent of the married couples had lived together, compared to only 19 percent in 1988. Of those couples whose partners were ages 50 to 64, 27 percent had cohabited.[4]

By May 2001, the proportion regarding premarital sex as wrong was only 40 percent; 57 percent, a clear majority, deemed it acceptable, up from only 21 percent in 1969. Only 47 percent of the American public believe it morally wrong for an unmarried woman to have a baby.[5]

Abortion

At this point some attention to the abortion controversy and the role of the morning-after pill in enhancing the sexual revolution is in order. Certainly, sex outside marriage became easier after these resources became legal and deemed legitimate birth-control techniques. Only a tiny minority of Americans (just 16 percent, according to a May 1999 Gallup poll) would advocate criminalizing abortion. The majority (55 percent) do favor some legal restrictions.[6]

Are these figures reflections of narcissism and the "grab for all the gusto you can" ethos of our era? My own reaction is to say "no." There has always been a significant core of women, those who would use a coat hanger in the back alley if they needed to, who along with their sympathetic men would support abortion under some circumstances. But even in this case, an appeal to some Augustinian wisdom helps.

Ultimately, the issue at stake is when human life begins. Indeed, when abortion is countenanced by those still believing that human life begins at conception, I share the pro-life critique. Arguments in support of abortion on grounds of right to choose are really about self-fulfillment and narcissism. Not only are they symptomatic of problematic social currents in America, but they will serve only to continue to make abortion a divisive issue in American society. In the final analysis, pro-abortion and pro-life segments of the population will be able to communicate significantly only if both sides conduct dialogue on the issue of whether abortion is the termination of a human life. Introducing an Augustinian perspective on that matter can channel the passions on each side into a real community effort. The dialogue on abortion could begin to focus the public's attention away from name-calling and the demonization of opponents and toward a sophisticated philosophical debate on the nature of human life (as this matter needs to be resolved in order to determine whether the unborn fetus is a human life).

An Augustinian perspective in this debate would inject a healthy skepticism. Participants in the debate about human life would be reminded that no formula or scientific data contains all the truth. Indeed an Augustinian perspective urges us to keep the dialogue going, since we can never be too cock-sure about the truth of our favorite positions. But while we continue this important, more edifying debate about the nature of human life, the realism of Augustinian thinking would inject one more element that both sides need to consider. This is a piece of wisdom about abortion that street-wise women have always known. (My mother taught it to me in adolescence.) "Men can make all the laws they want prohibiting abortion, but a girl can always get one." Anti-abortion legislation never has and never will put an end to abortions.

If we could inject this sort of Augustinian perspective into the public dialogue about abortion, it could make a similar contribution to the debate on related issues, like the validity of stem-cell research and human cloning. Like the issue of abortion's validity, the position we take on stem-cell research and human cloning presupposes a certain view of the nature of human life, of what constitutes a human being. Augustinianism will not solve these matters. But it gets us looking in the right directions with a healthy dose of self-criticism and tolerance for the ones with whom we disagree.

Homosexuality

This is another issue provoking no less tendentious discourse that might be dealt with more fruitfully from an Augustinian perspective than with the therapeutic or civil rights discourse by which it is presently characterized. The real issue in dispute, I submit, is whether homosexuality is natural. And although there is some evidence that some animals do engage in homosexual behavior and that there are differences in the brain structures of homosexuals and heterosexuals, the question of whether it is natural (from a Christian perspective of whether God created humans that way) remains an open, debatable question. In addition to the common-sense observation that sexual organs seem to be primarily for the purpose of procreation, conclusions have been drawn by some researchers that because human love is the result of chemical reactions in the body, homosexuality may result from a biochemical anomaly that occurs during fetal development.[7] In considering these matters, we need the self-criticism and tolerance that Augustine can teach. Just as it does in the case of abortion, the Augustinian perspective urges us to keep the dialogue going, since we can never be sure that our own position has not been illicitly influenced by our selfish desires. And what we desire is not always good for us or society. We need to have our "truths" confronted by other perspectives in a community dialogue in order for something close to truth to emerge.

In any case, since the 1970s, when the gay movement succeeded in promoting homosexuality as a civil rights issue, being gay and lesbian (or at least not bashing practitioners of homosexuality) has become politically correct. In most states sodomy laws are off the books. To be sure, the AIDS epidemic and the homophobia surrounding it did not enhance the drive for gay rights. But the drive toward the full legal recognition of gay unions has made significant headway, notably with their legalization in Vermont. In American religion, as we noted, the push is on for the ordination of practicing homosexuals in the liberal and mainline communities, and most of them long ago ceased condemning the gay lifestyle. As in the case of abortion, the American public is more open-minded on this issue than many of its spokespersons. According to Gallup polls, by 1999, 50 percent of the public favored legalizing homosexuality, a nearly eight-point increase since 1977.[8]

It is precisely at this point that injecting an Augustinian perspective into the debate is so crucial. As in the case of abortion, a healthy skepticism about the latest scientific findings regarding homosexuality is good for keeping the debate alive. Also, as we have noted, an Augustinian perspective reminds us of the need to keep the dialogue going. It can get us closer to something like the truth.

The New Realities Regarding Marriage and Raising Kids: Doing What's Good for Business

Census figures reveal that although in 1960, 45 percent of American families had two parents in the home with children, in 2000 only 20 percent of families had that status. Between 1970 and 2000, the number of single mothers rose from 3 million to 10 million, and single fathers now number 2 million, up from only 393,000 in 1970.[9] This is both good news (for business) and bad news.

The new way of doing family, with more single parents, is better for business on at least two levels. The more women in the workforce, the more workers. Business always does better with a large labor force. The more the labor force has to compete for jobs, the less business needs to pay workers, and the less pressure there is for paying benefits. In addition, the single-parent family is more flexible, more open to job relocation, precisely what contemporary business demands of its labor force.

Business also benefits from single parenthood from the standpoint of cultivating consumers. Divorce creates more households, and the more households, the more consumption, and so the better for business.

The marked increase in divorces and the fragility of contemporary marriage have already been noted. Certainly the narcissist stress on immediate gratification has contributed to these pressures. But the contemporary business ethos, with its demand for flexibility and increased working hours, also pressures marriages.

More hours on the job, separating couples, means less time together to build a relationship and more opportunities for resentment, not to mention temptation. If I spend more time with my colleagues of the opposite sex than I do with my spouse, if I share more with them than with my spouse, then the marriage relationship is diminished—and opportunities for mischief may arise. A business culture that rewards my flexibility does nothing to encourage my loyalty to my spouse if these opportunities emerge.

Marriages today are also more brittle because of the higher expectations placed on them.[10] Since the advent of romantic love in the fifteenth or sixteenth century and its widespread popularization in the nineteenth century, we have come to expect that our spouse provide us with all sorts of tingly feelings. In the last decades, though, the difference has been that now we are apt to look for such feelings through new relationships when the natural hormonal reactions of familiarity set in.[11]

A little bit of Augustinian, biological realism by way of digression is in order at this point. Love is increasingly being shown to be related to the chemicals the body secretes when members of the opposite sex are attracted to each other. Each partner is flooded with chemical cousins of amphetamines, notably the chemical phenylethylamine. The highs provided by these chemicals do not last. As with any amphetamine, the body builds up a tolerance, which means it requires more phenylethylamine to keep the romantic high. After two or three years the body no longer secretes enough of the chemical to provide the romantic high, which explains why passionate love cools. Of course, other chemicals, like oxytocin, take the place of these amphetamines, but they produce different kinds of pleasurable reactions, like the desire to snuggle or a sense of security and calm.[12]

Science has here confirmed what Augustine knew all along, that human love is selfish love. We love because it feels good.

What our therapeutic, narcissist climate has effectively done is convinced large segments of the public that the short-term high is better than long-term feelings of peace and security. A flexible economy nurtures desires for flexibility.

Related to these dynamics is the pressure many men have begun to feel as a result of post-1960s social acceptance of women seeking sexual fulfillment.[13] An Augustinian appreciation that such lust undergirds all we do would make this not so surprising and would help both the performance-pressured men and their desirous partners to realize that not every encounter will satisfy everyone. Further, it's the phenylethylamine and the subsequent more calming chemicals secreted that count more than a single encounter.

The unwillingness of large segments of Western culture (for the divorce epidemic is widespread also in European nations) and of the American public in particular to weather the hormonal changes that come with committed relationships, egged on by our social narcissism and its therapeutic ethos, has had serious social consequences. These trends have had especially unhappy implications for the African-American community. They are more pronounced in this subculture, and they tend to exacerbate the likelihood of a Black family falling into or remaining in poverty.

While in 1960 two-thirds of Black children lived in two-parent homes (compared to 91 percent of White children), by 1995 the percentage had shrunk to one-third, compared to 76 percent of Whites. In 1960 only 22 percent of births to Black women were out of wedlock. By 1994 that figure was 70 percent. Likewise, while in 1960 only 28 percent of Black women between 15 and 45 had never been married, by 1998 the figure was more than 50 percent.[14]

Such single motherhood entails a higher likelihood of poverty among Blacks than Whites. The increased poverty makes the success of marriage in the Black community, especially in its impoverished segments, less likely. Without the economic security of the husband's having a good, steady job, marriage seems less like a good deal for the Black woman. The pressures of racism on the Black man have led some to claim a kind of macho attitude, which some African-American women have found problematic, particularly in view of the self-reliance that the Black woman has tended to display since slavery.

The pressures placed on contemporary marriage yearn for healthy doses of Augustinian realism. Our exploration of contemporary biological insights teaches couples to expect some altering of the initial passions. When we clear away from our eyes the cult of celebrity glamour and Enlightenment optimism, when we take the biological insights noted here more seriously than we do romantic pop psychology, it becomes evident that altering of passions in a marriage is healthy and normal. Wonderful as marriage is, the married state, like any human relation, has its trials. We are reminded of Augustine's words regarding marriage, which were cited in the first chapter, his contention that even marriage and parenting bring misery, for even "the home, the natural refuge from the ills of life, is itself not safe."[15] We need to get that word out in American society. Such (biologically verified) realism is good for the institution of marriage.

We have previously noted that ours is not a child-friendly society. It is also unfriendly to the elderly. Such discrimination is hardly surprising, given the narcissist and therapeutic preoccupation with self-fulfillment and immediate gratification that is in the social air we breathe today. This prioritizing of the "now" involves a break with historical continuity, which also manifests in an ageism that devalues the elderly and promotes a cult of youth, pressuring the middle-aged to put off aging as long as possible. (Of course, the neglect of the elderly may change with the mass of narcissism-oriented Baby Boomers retiring in the next two decades.)

The vulnerability of children is a more pressing problem. While in 1970 some 10.2 million children were below the poverty level (14.9 percent of American children), by 1998, 12.8 million children (18.3 percent of the population) fell into this category.[16] Each year, one million children suffer homelessness.[17]

The staggering statistics reported in 2000 by the National Center on Child Abuse and Neglect are relevant. As recently as

1998, almost 3 million children (one in twenty-three) were alleged victims of maltreatment.[18] We also see the neglect of children in the statistics on "deadbeat dads." While according to 1997 government statistics 6.3 million American men not living with their children were liable for child support, only 2.6 million of them actually paid. Statistics were even worse by 2000, as nearly 9.9 million fathers refused to pay full child support assessments.[19]

Although it has not been "politically correct" to lament the impact of divorce on children in cases where the parents are White and at least middle-class, a new study by eminent psychologist E. Mavis Hetherington raises interesting issues. Her study discloses that 75 percent to 80 percent of such children grow up to function effectively. But only a small percentage had good relations with their fathers, and few were happily married. In addition, while only 10 percent of the children from intact families have serious social, emotional, or psychological problems, 25 percent of children from divorced families exhibit these problems. The toll of divorce on even economically secure children with successful parents—a toll in their psyche, trust level, and spirit of adventure—seems documented by this study and by observations of other analysts.[20]

Even in functional two-parent families, parenting has fallen on hard times in American society. As with marriage and the other problems identified, this is related to the optimistic understanding of human nature, for such a view of human nature undergirds much contemporary parenting ideology. We have assumed that what children most need to become well-adjusted adults is self-respect, and we want to be their "friends."[21] Note how the assumption is that fundamentally good children will develop into healthy adults without much help, as long as we do not get in the way. (Of course, we also insist that they respect the "needs" of adults.) Thus we count "quality time" as more valuable than quantity of time, as if children were good enough to raise themselves most of the time, with just a little bit of "quality" help from adults.

These dynamics have roots in the 1930s and 1940s, when a stress on the insight of therapy to improve parenting began to undermine parental confidence. The results have been permissiveness and an opening for a whole new market for business in clothes, vitamins, cereals, etc.[22] The impact of the therapeutic and business models on contemporary American society is again evident.

Also note how the lack of parental confidence feeds the marketing of youth culture businesses. Instead of focusing on guiding children, recent clinical models of parenting like Parent Effectiveness Training urge adults only to "hear" the feelings of their children. As a result today's parents often spend a lot of time not leading, because they are struggling to "keep up with the kids," to master their jargon and even their fashions.[23]

Other contemporary social dynamics have had striking impact on parenting styles and the children we raise. There can be no denying that the increase of women in the workforce has been at the expense of children, this by the unwitting confirmation of the women involved. As early as the 1970s, 66 percent of American adults surveyed agreed that "parents should be free to live their own lives even if it means spending less time with their children." Of course such attitudes were in the air, as women were advised by cultural gurus of the era that they dare not make children more important than themselves.[24] Christopher Lasch has observed that such a parenting ethos betrays an emotional coolness to children that is likely to nurture another generation of self-empty narcissists.[25]

With increased numbers of women in the workforce, the use of day care for children has skyrocketed. Indeed, leaving one's children to others has become a test of one's commitment to female independence and equality.[26] In 1999, 54 percent of American children from birth to third grade were in child care.[27] It seems to be the politically correct thing to do, for mothers are said to need to have the fulfillment of a career (and besides, as we have noted, it is good for business).

Regarding this feel-good, no-guilt shifting of responsibility for child care to (sometimes unqualified, untrained) providers, a recent study by University of London professor of psychology Jay Belsky was most controversial. He claimed that his study of children in such facilities in comparison with those raised by stay-at-home mothers revealed that children spending much time in day care are three times as likely to be aggressive as children whose mothers cared for them at home.

One of the significant, but largely ignored, presuppositions of welfare reform and government policy pertains to the mandate that welfare recipients work outside the home. Thus, while only 33 percent of single mothers with children had a job in 1993, the figure grew to 44 percent in five years (by 1998).[28] Is that entirely something to celebrate, that larger numbers of children on welfare spend the day apart from a parent? A 2002 proposal by George Bush to increase the welfare work requirement from thirty to forty hours would further add to the time that mothers spend away from their children. Does this constitute family values, or is it punishing the poor and nurturing a larger constituency of aggressive offspring of the impoverished?

Other statistics pertaining to the nation's children may also be relevant to this discussion of prevailing patterns of parenting and what sort of priorities our government sets. Experimentation with marijuana is on the rise again among America's children. According to a recent survey conducted by the National Institute on Drug Abuse, while in 1992 some 21.9 percent of high school seniors had smoked marijuana, the proportion climbed to 37.5 percent by 1998 and continued to remain at that level through 2001. There has been a corresponding decline among eighth-, tenth-, and twelfth-graders of the belief that smoking pot is dangerous.[29] Could the prevailing methods of child-rearing be a factor in this development?

The school shootings are an even more dramatic indication of the decline of quality of life for children in America. Some kids today go to school afraid of what might happen.

A 1999 survey conducted by the U.S. Department of Education revealed that the average American child between the ages of two and eighteen spends 1,500 hours annually watching TV. What should be highlighted in this context is that children of this age average a mere 75 hours annually talking to parents. It's a lot easier to baby-sit the kids with TV and computers than to talk to them or play with them.

Of course this neglect is balanced by a permissiveness and an obsessive concern to get just the right things for our children—the right educational toys, the right schools, placement on the right athletic teams and in the best music programs and summer camps, etc. This sort of obsessiveness about scheduling our children's activities (in part because such activities alleviate the parents of child-care responsibilities) may also relate to the current interest in year-round schools. A 2002 University of Michigan study revealed that free time has decreased in a child's day, from 40 percent of the day devoted to free play in 1981 to only 24 percent in 1997. Americans seem to have a hang-up about structuring the lives of their children. Permissiveness undergirds such obsessions. It also became a watchword in the schools and was popularized in the late 1970s by the English baby guru Penelope Leach, who claimed that the word "no" crushes children's self-esteem.[30] Note again how the therapeutic agenda provides a guiding paradigm for much of what is transpiring in society today.

There is an interesting paradox here: the indulgence of parents and their neglect of their children in terms of time and supervision. It is not so hard to understand. One word explains it: GUILT. If I'm not spending time with my kids like I should, if I'm not always there to supervise them or at their games, at least I can indulge them with money and high-powered activities. Social commentator David Frum also has a valid explanation of these dynamics. He wrote:

> Indulgence follows neglect as surely as hangovers follow booze. . . . But this sort of obsessiveness [typical of today's parents] flows much more from the parents' own ego than from the needs of the child. There was much talk in the 1970s of how male sexual hunger transformed women into objects. Parental obsessiveness can do the same to children.[31]

There is also an interesting downside to the near-obsessive concern of many of today's parents with scheduling their children in just the right activities. As we noted with regard to youth programs, today's children and recent college graduates have lost some ability to organize themselves in their own activities just for the sake of fun. A number of today's youth even attribute the decline of dating on college campuses in favor of the only two social options in town—free sex ("hooking up") or living together—to the lack of opportunity to organize their own social lives during adolescence.[32] To the degree that there is any truth to these reflections, it is a damning critique of the way most middle-class parents are raising their kids.

Let us not idealize parental love in any context, as too many of today's parents so intent on managing their children's lives are wont to do. Even parental love at its best has elements of selfishness. The great American Reformed theologian Reinhold Niebuhr said it well in a 1961 sermon:

> The love of parents for their children is a virtuous going out from ourselves. It is one of the ways of grace that overcomes our selfishness; that we fall in love, that we love our families, that we love our mates and we love our children. We think we are virtuous. Looking at our virtue, we say, "I am a good parent." Probably we are not as good as we think we are. Our children may not have the same complacent judgment about us. And they may be good children, they may not be even rebellious. They are just trying to establish themselves, and they detect, without being psychiatrists, that there is a curious combination of possessiveness with our love, particularly if we are good parents.[33]

Parents need some Augustinian realism, and the good ones already have it. It's hardly surprising after all that we would be possessive with our kids' lives. It makes biological common sense. In loving them, we are loving our genes. Never forget, then, that parental love is as such a selfish love, for in loving our offspring we love ourselves.

Augustinian Common Sense about Sex, Marriage, and Family

What might happen if American parents had a self-understanding like Augustine and James Madison regarding their own "needs" and how the fulfillment of parental pride is a manifestation of self-interest, hubris, and concupiscence? If we could blow the whistle on ourselves when we are organizing our children's activities or defending their "rights" and preferences in the face of the exercise of valid authority by other adults over them, if we kept an eye on our egos as much as possible, we would probably be a little more effective parents.

The adoption of this realistic, common-sense view of human nature also entails a renewed appreciation of the fact that children are not innocent and devoid of selfishness. Consequently, they will not grow up to be responsible citizens if left to their own devices. Children need consistent discipline and instruction in values. These insights are also relevant for our educational system, as shall be discussed below. Would the result of American society's widespread appropriation of such Augustinian insights mean that more children would grow up in stable, happy homes?

An Augustinian view of parenting concedes the inevitability of our failures. It also recognizes that with hard work, love, and some miracles, kids can still turn out well. One sixteenth-century Augustinian, Martin Luther, summarized the matter powerfully, insisting that when a child turns out good it really is a miracle, the work of God:

> It still happens to many parents that their children turn out to be bad—even when they have had good training. God does not want us to give them free rein and to grant them their will. . . . If our efforts are successful, we should thank God; if not, we have at least done our part. For that children turn out to be good does not lie in our power and might, but it is God's. If He is not in the ship with us, we shall never sail smoothly.[34]

This Augustinian insight can lift the weight, make parenting more fun. When parents realize that they cannot do it all, they can become a little less obsessive. Augustinian Christians are people who know that parenting is nothing more than the joyous experience of being a vehicle of the will of God, not really of determining who their kids are or will be.

Our discussion of sex and marriage also requires some closing consideration of the issues raised by the women's liberation and gay liberation movements. We have noted that the American public as a whole is supportive of these movements to the extent that they seek to establish equal rights. What needs to happen next is to examine to what degree the peripheral issues associated with these movements (women in the workforce and the legal recognition of homosexual relationships) are in fact good for society. But as long as we examine these movements from the perspective of an Enlightenment optimism, believing that all people and their motives are fundamentally good, or with the therapeutic mindset, embracing the supposition that what is good for a woman's or a practicing gay's self-fulfillment is good for America, we will never get around to raising important questions for the sake of the common good. Such questions will continue to be perceived as "politically incorrect" as long as Enlightenment optimism and the therapeutic outlook continue to be the only dominant worldviews in town.

The Augustinian view of human nature and its correlated Madisonian view of self-interested factions remind the American public that abuses can emerge even in special interest groups no matter how righteous the cause. Have we looked at the economic implications of giving gay couples the tax breaks available to heterosexual married couples, but not to single heterosexual friends of the same gender who live together? Have we considered the costs of a social ethos that makes it seem that women who elect to stay home with children are not liberated? Until we rehabilitate Augustine's as a widely recognized viewpoint, these questions will not be part of the public debate. They will be perceived as too uncaring or reactionary to receive serious attention from the cultural elites.

I have already suggested how reviving the Augustinian viewpoint could be good for heterosexual marriage by helping Americans become more realistic about the institution. Again the sixteenth-century Augustinian Martin Luther puts the point so well:

> As I have said, the best way to prevent divorce and other discord is for everyone to learn patience in putting up with common faults . . . knowing that we can never have everything just right, the way we would like to have it. Even the condition of your own body can never be any different or better. You have to put up with the many kinds of filth and discomfort that it causes you every day. . . . You make allowances for all this. In fact, this only increases your concern and love for your body; you wait on it and wash it, and you endure and help in every way you can. Why not do the same with the spouse whom God has given you, who is an even greater treasure and whom you have even more reason to love?[35]

Benjamin Franklin, an American founder with similar Augustinian dispositions, put it this way: "You can bear your own Faults, and why not a Fault in your Wife."[36]

For all its ups and downs, there is statistical evidence that lifelong marriage is a wonderful, joyful affair. In his appeal for reestablishing more social connections among narcissist Americans, public policy expert Robert Putnam provided polling information that indicates that married people are much happier than the unmarried. In fact, statistically, the effect of marriage on life is equivalent to moving roughly seventy percentiles up the income hierarchy (and richer people poll as happier).[37] These statistics do not negate the likelihood that this happiness is realistic in its outlook. Given what is at stake for society and individuals in preserving long-term marriage, we need to work harder at exposing popular culture to this Augustinian realism about the institution, to expect a few hassles along with all the unspeakable joys.

seven

Augustinian Common Sense in the American Classroom

The well-documented decline of the American educational system is common knowledge. Once again, this social problem is related to the optimistic and illusory understanding of human nature that undergirds much modern educational theory.

Public education is under fire, but the American university system has its problems too. Regarding the former, we hear political rhetoric about privatizing it (turning our schools over to businesses to administer them). And vouchers to permit parents to remove their children from underperforming schools and allow them instead to attend private schools financed by tax dollars have now even been deemed constitutional by the Supreme Court. The home-school movement is also being mounted as a reaction against the decline of the American school system. An estimated one million children are being home-schooled today. And there seems to be success. Home-schoolers beat public- and private-school students by an average eighty-one points on the SAT.

Not enough attention has been given to the flaws of these alternatives. The home-schooled student, like the private-school student, is somewhat restricted from the full experience of childhood. As with the narcissist dynamics of the middle-class subdivision and the modern city, the child never experiences

seven159

the full diversity of community life. Like the narcissists, home-schooled children are effectively taught by their mode of education that institutions can be redesigned to fit "chosen" lifestyles. This is in marked contrast to the public-school experience from which children learn (sometimes painfully) that some aspects of life are chaotically given. Which of these ways of nurturing children will lead to the happiest, richest life?

Similar flaws characterize the prospects of a voucher system, which seems to underline the narcissist ethos of our time. Again the child is led to think that there are ways out of tough situations that do not meet needs, rather than to learn that with discipline and hard work one can overcome bad situations. As for privatizing the educational system, this seems to be another example of the attempt of business to dominate every sphere of our lives. If business is in charge of our schools, could we not expect a conflict of interests over curricular matters? More so than is already the case, would not our schools become more oriented to the agenda of what best prepares the next generation of workers, and less and less oriented to the humanities and the goal of producing learned people, knowledgeable citizens?

The Failure of the American Public School System

Certainly there are reasons to seek alternatives to our present situations. There are data that seem to indicate the failure of our public school system. There was a notable decline in SAT scores from 1963 until the last decade. In 1963 the average score for the verbal portion of the test was 478, and 502 for the math portion. These scores contrast markedly with later ones, which show an almost 17 percent decline in verbal scores and a 10 percent decline in math scores through the 1960s and 1970s. Since 1990 scores have been higher (an average of 506 for verbal and 514 for math in 2001), but the increase does not tell the whole story. It belies the fact that until 1990 the criteria for computing scores were based on the average scores of those taking the test in 1941. Today the computation criterion is the average of those who took the exams in 1990. The 1941 group was a more elite and college-bound group than the more representative sample who took the exams in 1990. Thus today's scores are based on a norm drawn from students who would not have performed as well on the exams as those whose tests determined the SAT scores of those taking College Boards before 1990. Though the numbers on SAT tests are higher than they were in the last thirty years, should we conclude that the performance of students has gone down, since scores seem to be based on lower criteria? While not making the test easier, have we effectively "dumbed down" SAT scores?

Gloomy statistics abound. Recent results of the Third International Mathematics and Science Study indicated that eighth-grade American children educated in our schools ranked twenty-fifth worldwide in science and nineteenth in mathematics. Their peers in Singapore, the Czech Republic, and Japan headed the list, with those from the Netherlands (ranking sixth) leading all the Western nations. Particularly startling was that U.S. fourth-graders ranked seventh internationally. Thus the American school system seems to be developing inferior students, at least in math. The longer they stay in school, the worse they become in relation to their peers.

The results of the more recent, congressionally mandated National Assessment of Educational Progress revealed similar data. According to a 2000 test, only 25 percent of fourth-graders, 26 percent of eighth-graders, and 17 percent of twelfth-graders were at or below grade level in math. Nearly three-fourths of American students fall below expectations, and the longer they stay in high school, the more they fall behind.

What are the causes of these failures? Like most social problems, they have complex causes. Yet we can readily identify certain trends that are typical of our other social ills.

There was a period, until the recent preoccupation with standardized testing, when most contemporary education was dominated by the therapeutic paradigm. The overriding agenda was to encourage the creativity of students and to make them feel good about themselves. A glaring example of this approach to education was the introduction of the whole-language approach. The basic supposition of this method is to permit students to write how they feel, without reference to grammatical rules. Obviously, it has not worked, as American children, today's college students trained with this method, do not know how to write. Clearly, an optimistic view of human nature hovers in the background of this approach. Thus, the therapeutic paradigm also stands in the background.

Certainly the therapeutic model is evidenced in the decline of discipline in many public schools. Visit an American classroom, and you will notice that the kids are a lot noisier and get away with a lot more than they did twenty years ago. Administrators' offices are often not the place of the most fearsome punishment, as transpired in days of old. Frequently the problem child is instead referred to the school counselor.[1]

Social promotion is another example of the impact of therapy on the educational system. Though it is currently being reconsidered in many school districts under the pressures of the standardized-test movement, it is still very much in play. Children are advanced even though they have not demonstrated the necessary intellectual competence, because not to advance them with their peers would be bad for their self-esteem and social development.

Indeed the optimistic view of human nature is presupposed throughout much of the curriculum of American education. Thus we have assumed that children are innately curious and creative, that they want to learn and are not biased by their surroundings, that they will become well-adjusted adults as long as we do not undermine their self-respect.

This failure of our schools has an impact on the worldview and outlook of their products. Inadvertently, the schools tend to feed the narcissistic trends already in our society. Allan Bloom captured this mode well in a 1987 book. Characterizing today's American student, the product of public schools, he wrote:

> Because their poor education has impoverished their longing . . .
> what they do have is an unordered tangle of rather ordinary pas-

sions, running though their consciousness like a monochrome kaleidoscope. They are egoists, not in a vicious way, not in the way of those who know the good, just or noble, and selfishly reject them, but because the ego is all there is in present theory, in what they are taught.[2]

When all you learn is about yourself, studying everything in light of your experience or its utility, you lose a richness in what you hope for and dream about.

Public Opinion

All is not lost for public schools regarding the American public's desire to trust them. Fully 50.9 percent of those asked in a federal government inquiry claimed to have a great deal or quite a lot of confidence in the school system (ranking it behind only religious organizations and the American university system).[3] Yet concern about the school system still runs high. A July 2001 Gallup poll showed that Americans deem it the second most important problem in the country, only slightly behind concern with the economy. Earlier it had been running second to ethics/morality/religion/family decline.[4]

The public, spurred on by politicians and the media, tends to blame the educational establishment for the problems. Teachers are the villains. In his acclaimed book *The Schools We Need: Why We Don't Have Them,* University of Virginia scholar E. D. Hirsch claimed that for the last seventy-five years American education has been in the stranglehold of an educational establishment that has prioritized learning dynamics and developmental theories over the accumulation of knowledge.

Columnist John Leo's more recent analysis of the curricula of education departments that train teachers provides numerous disturbing examples of how saturated they are with the therapeutic paradigm. Student papers in education courses typically concern student feelings about teaching, and the prospective educators are discouraged from exercising authority in the classroom.[5] In view of the impact that the strategies of whole-language theory and social promotion have had on American education, it seems that both Hirsch and Leo had a point.

There is no question that the status of the teaching profession has been in decline since the middle of the twentieth century. And there *are* bad teachers. But are they all bad? The public is perhaps not ready to hear this message, but we need to examine the role of parents in the decline of education. We have already observed that in the last thirty years the model for parenting has been permissiveness and indulgence, and how the two go together. Certainly, the public has acknowledged that there has been a decline in parenting since the seventies. A Gallup poll taken in 1998 indicated that 67 percent of the public believed that parents did a worse job then than ever before. Only 4 percent believed that parenting had improved.[6] And there is a growing recognition, at least among the opinion makers, that parents expect the schools to do more for them (witness the rise of after-school care programs) and to do the parenting in the same indulgent style that they practice. Here lies what may be the core problem with our schools, the one that our politicians and the analysts want to dodge: it has to do with the attitudes and behaviors of the parents of today's school-aged children and the kids they (sort of) raise.

The generally accepted supposition about the role of parents in education is that the more involvement, the better. There is some real truth to this "common wisdom." Too many parents today do not check their children's homework and follow their academic progress. If the parents don't care, the kids won't work. These dynamics help account for the inability of many impoverished communities successfully to educate their children for the workplace, and so break the cycle of poverty. In such settings education does not matter to the majority of parents, and discipline is not taught. As a result, learning is a low priority for the children in these neighborhoods.

Another all-too-frequent response of today's parents, regardless of their economic status, is to complain about the workload assigned to their children. After all, "busy" parents do not want their evenings with their children interrupted by these activities. Overlooked in such narcissist, therapeutic thinking is that without discipline, learning does not take place. Education is not always fun; it's hard work.

Teachers and administrators, when they are frank, will report how much of a pest many parents can be. Many educational professionals report running scared of the parents. If they give "too much" homework or enforce standards, not just the kids (as has always been the case) but also their parents are likely to complain. We want high grades for our children (as do today's college students raised by such parents), but not with too much work.

Widespread reliance on private schools is not likely to solve this problem. In fact, standards in private education are likely to decline further if large numbers of children enroll in these schools and their unhappy parents begin to pressure the schools' instructors to reconsider their workload, reminding these educators that it is parents like them who pay their salaries. (The underachieving college-aged children of such parents are already delivering that line to their professors.)

The result of all this parental pressure has been that too many teachers have caved in, and so standards decline while grade inflation at even the best schools and Ivy League universities is on the rise. This dynamic began as early as the late 1970s, as documented by Berkeley professor Martin Trow. He noted that while in 1969 only 18 percent of college undergraduates reported a cumulative average of B+, by 1975, 36 percent reported a B+ average.[7] Though one dynamic in the increase of higher grades being awarded in this era was the faculty's desire to help students avoid the draft by staying in school, this was not the whole story. There are more recent indications that it is easier to graduate with a higher cumulative average these days than ever before, though the dynamics are different from mere grade inflation. The problem is the significant growth in the number of students dropping courses on college campuses (presumably after bombing a midterm exam and before a final exam). This dynamic, coupled with the larger number of repeated courses (in which case, only the higher grade received counts in the student's grade point average), swells the cumulative averages of the grades.[8]

No wonder our educational system is in disarray. It is not just the therapeutic bent of much of modern educational theory that accounts for the lower standards. As long as the desire for self-fulfillment of students and their parents prevails, standards will continue to deteriorate no matter how much standardized testing is introduced.

How What Helps Teaches Us What's Wrong

The negative impact of parental interference in the schools is borne out by a noteworthy 2000 report by the National Center for Educational Statistics. It revealed that 2000 test scores on the National Assessment of Educational Progress in Pentagon-run schools exceed the national average. Even the poorer students of these schools do better than the national average. Half the children in domestic-based schools qualify for free or reduced lunches, because their parents are low on the military pay scale. But 35 percent of these students still demonstrated writing proficiency on the standardized tests. This is close to the national rate of 40 percent, and far above the 10 percent rate of passing for all low-income students.[9]

Some commentators have suggested that the success of these schools lies in the ability of military commanders to hold parents accountable for their children's behavior and academic performance. Military bases also allow parents time off to participate in their children's school activities. My own suspicion is that the support that these parents must give the teachers is the most significant factor in the success of these schools. Military personnel do not challenge the authority of teachers in the base school. The kids, knowing that the teachers will be supported, have no choice but to work, because the usual excuses handed to parents will not work in their military context.

Is it time for the educational establishment to examine the success of these schools with an eye toward determining what makes them work? In order for real change to be made in our educational ethos, it must demand that the media and our politicians be willing to face the prospect of laying the blame on parents and on the therapeutic, narcissist impulses that shape their behavior and prevail throughout much of American society. But before exploring in more detail the realities of this approach, we should consider several other dynamics in the current educational system.

Should Education Be Run Like a Business?

The educational system, like almost every other American institution, has been lured into the business model. The stress on math and science over the humanities at every level of public and university education is a good example of business's seduction of American education. Especially in the computer age, math and science majors are more valuable to the business establishment than are history and English majors. Business does not need expertise in these disciplines. Thus we have a glut of Ph.D.s in these fields, with not enough university faculty positions available to them. On the other hand, the job markets are good in newly created departments of computer science.

Speaking of computers, the general uncritical endorsement of computer technology by the educational system also bespeaks the heavy influence of American business on our schools. Let us not be naive about how it is in the interests of business that schools produce computer-literate graduates, even if they do not know as much about Shakespeare, Socrates, or the underlying suppositions of the constitutional system of government as their predecessors did. Given these dynamics, it is hardly surprising that even universities have bought into these suppositions. Witness the establishment of departments of computer science even in old-line liberal arts institutions.

In a sense the influence of business on the educational system is of long-standing character. Public education began to adopt the business model in its older format in the middle of the twentieth century with the establishment of a far-ranging educational bureaucracy. Thus every school is part of a district with a central office, and at each school there are now four or five administrators. Everyone reports to the next higher level, right up to the federal government's Department of Education. What the bureaucratization of education has effectively accomplished is to divert more tax dollars to personnel outside the classroom while correspondingly undermining the teacher's autonomy. For administrators, not the teacher, must have the final say about curriculum and intellectual rigor, and sometimes even about specific cases of discipline.[10]

The business model is exhibiting more influence in several ways in the new push for longer school days and year-round schools. Long work days and short vacations (if any are granted at all) are the way of life in American business today. Can we understand the rationale for longer school days and year-round schools in any way other than as efforts to socialize correctly the next generation of workers? If it has to do with the desire to increase standards, why is there so much outcry among the present generation of parents about "excessive" homework given in the schools? It really has to do with the fact that working parents come home tired after a long day on the job and don't feel like spending time on homework. Besides, after dropping the kids off in day care, the guilt begins in such a way that parents would rather take the time together with the kids to play with them than be the "cop" who ensures that the homework gets done.

Other dynamics related to business are involved in the push for longer school days and year-round school. In families where no one is home to greet the kids after school or take care of them during the long summer vacation (because big business needs mothers in the workforce), these new school schedules can take care of the day-care problem. That is good for business, because with the new push for on-site day care, using the schools can be a lot cheaper.

For all its good intentions to raise standards, the emphasis on standardized testing is another manifestation of the business model's impact on American education. In business, success is clearly measurable by performance or results (the bottom line). Longtime educators tend to agree that success in education is not so readily measured. But the paradigm that underlies the standardized-test movement is the measuring of performance or outcomes. Should business models call the shots in our schools?

Other abuses of the standardized-test movement need to be noted. Teaching to the tests is an inevitable temptation. Teaching will be directed to questions likely to be posed on the test rather than to the broad spectrum of a subject's material. Time that could be spent on instruction in the subject is wasted explaining test-taking strategies.

There is one other dimension of the current crisis in our public schools that demands our attention. I refer to the growing teacher shortage. Especially with the large generation born after the early 1980s now flooding our schools, as well as the impending early retirement of baby-boom generation teachers, the shortage is reaching crisis proportions. And only about one-half the number of American university graduates entered the field of teaching in 1997 as graduated with an education degree in 1971.[11] The situation is exacerbated even further by the high level of dropouts from the teaching profession. Almost one-half of new teachers leave the profession in the first five years.

It is unfair to blame these dynamics on the business community and its influence on the public school system. The self-indulgence of parents who regularly hassle teachers when they do not get what they want is a factor. But the dominance of the business community in contemporary American society does play a contributing role in the teacher shortage.

First, in a society where business leaders are the most admired people and the ones who have jobs with the greatest financial rewards, the teaching profession will not draw candidates in large numbers. Also, the era of big business and its crusade against big government, and the corresponding call for cutting taxes, has made less money available for teacher salaries.

Finally, not to be discounted in the high attrition rate among teachers is the educational establishment's adoption of business-management techniques that entail the regular filing of endless reports to document their professional activities for the ever-growing ranks of administrators. In view of the broadening influence of the standardized-test movement and the correlated growing preoccupation of governmental and accreditation agencies with outcomes-based educational theory (mandating that schools document improved performance by students), the paper-trail demands are likely to grow even larger. The ranks of disappointed teachers who entered the profession to work with kids and who are not turned on by administrative duties are likely to grow.

The business of education is not business, primarily to be about preparing the next generation of the workforce. Nor can its primary agenda be to nurture character and self-respect, and it certainly cannot be to teach religion. Of course, as was previously discussed, were we to restore an appreciation of the Augustinian vision of the Constitution among today's students and in the culture in general, if the Christian roots of these suppositions were clarified in accord with Supreme Court's blessing of the teaching of religious views presented descriptively,[12] then a lot of the cries by segments of the population against the separation of church and state could be addressed. If education is merely about factual information, it fails the students, because then they have not learned how to think. But if all we do is promote creativity without factual information, then graduates have nothing to think with.

The preceding observations reflect a very constitutionally-oriented perspective on the educational system. As with any institution, when one faction's agenda prevails there is sure to be chaos or tyranny. The self-interested character of factions guarantees that. Institutions work best when there is a creative interplay of various perspectives. Thus the Augustine in me urges a school system in which there is an ongoing interplay of all these agendas—those of the parents, of professional educators, of the nation (educating good citizens who love the nation), and even of business. There is even a place for the interplay between content, creativity, and the feeling agenda of the therapeutic ethos. We shall return to this point in closing.

Politically Correct University Life

Predictably, the American system of higher education has been affected by trends that are reflected in our public schools. Commentators have lamented the decline of the caliber of university life since the early 1960s. Today's undergraduates—products of the American public education system that they are—simply are not as well prepared intellectually or emotionally for the rigors of a high-quality university education as were previous generations. On the whole, the ethos of the twenty-first-century American university does not do much to overcome their lack of preparedness.

We have already noted how a kind of grade inflation has hit college campuses, with a dynamic different from but not unrelated to the higher grades awarded today in public schools. Attend a graduation and note the number of cum laude graduates; it is hard to believe, given the way that SAT scores have had to be recalculated in order to keep them from declining.

Dropping requirements in favor of a curriculum primarily comprised of electives or in favor of requirements more geared to the faculty's research interests has been disastrous. The consequences for a literate public have also been disastrous. A 1999 survey of college seniors at fifty-five elite colleges (including the Ivy League) revealed that only 44 percent knew that Lincoln was president between 1860 and1880, 25 percent thought the Pilgrims signed the Magna Carta, and 63 percent did not know about the Battle of the Bulge. At the time of the survey, none of these colleges required a course in American history, and 78 percent did not require any course in history.[13]

Some commentators are not sure that having the classical general-education requirements still in place would matter, given the lack of preparation of incoming students and the business ethos that has dominated their upbringing and the campus ethos. Students attend college to prepare for a good job. In a sense this is nothing new. Higher education as the path to a better life has been part of the great American dream since the large-scale nineteenth-century creation of church-related colleges. What has changed, according to political scientist Allan Bloom, is that today's students are narrower and "flatter" than earlier generations. Perhaps because of the decline of reading in favor of the instant gratification of TV and computer virtual reality, significant numbers of today's youth may have lost the ability to yearn. Books that stimulate imagination nurture yearning. If you've seen it all, been exposed to all the realities, and are used to instant gratification, you do not yearn as much. The result, Bloom concludes, is that the majority of today's college students are more content with the state of affairs (the media has effectively marketed its worldview to them) and also more discontented and despairing of ever escaping what is (because there seems to be nothing more to yearn for that they can imagine).[14]

There is also a new kind of elitism on college campuses, reflected in both the faculty and the student body. America's prestigious colleges have so raised tuition that they have largely returned to being bastions of the sons and daughters of the rich, with scholarships available only to the children of impoverished minority families. The middle class is being effectively squeezed out, just as it has been squeezed in other economic and social ways.[15]

Elitism reflects in the faculty ethos of American colleges. In an increasingly tight job market, the humanities and social sciences faculty have been pressured in the last decades like never before to "publish or perish." The sort of books and journal articles that are produced, though, are for audiences of other specialists, not for general readers. In fact, if you write too much for the general readers, you are likely to be branded a "popularizer," to the detriment of your tenure prospects. As a result, much of the scholarship of the American academy has given up communicating with the public. Of course, with the advent of television and the computer, given the sort of surface-level communication we have seen these media best propagate, even popular books on substantive topics would not likely make much of a dent in popular opinion. This estrangement of scholars from the general public further exacerbates the sense of elitism on American campuses.

These dynamics have likewise contributed to widening the gap between students and faculty. The sort of research publishing faculty need to do to survive in the guild is so specialized as not typically to be relevant to undergraduates or even to graduate students. Teaching core courses becomes more a nuisance to faculty, a task increasingly turned over to graduate assistants. In addition, the pressure of publishing and the rewards for it render faculty less and less likely to be available for informal dialogue with and instruction of students.

In a paradoxical way the estrangement between scholarship and certain segments of the general public is not as complete as it seems. Indeed there is a sense in which the academy has become so identified with the American social trends, so ensconced in "political correctness," that it can no longer be an effective countercultural voice.

In its golden years, just after World War II through the 1960s, the American university was undergoing an intellectual revolution that has had a profound impact on American society. Allan Bloom has provided a persuasive analysis of these developments.[16] Essentially, his point is that the Germans may have lost the war, but their Enlightenment-era scholars won the hearts and minds of American scholars and eventually American popular culture. For it was in this era that the relativism initiated by the German Enlightenment philosopher Immanuel Kant, with his distinction between the noumenon (the Thing-in-Itself) and the phenomenon (one's perception of the noumenal reality), began to make a dent on the American social psyche.[17] Essentially, this scheme entails that all our knowledge is relative to the individual's perception of it. Given Kantian suppositions, we can never achieve knowledge in itself, objective knowledge.

Kant's philosophy began to influence German and European thought quite early. The implied relativism, having the interpreter's experience function as the starting point for all that we know and say, is in the background of the theological approach that Friedrich Schleiermacher evolved, and we have already noted how profoundly influential it has been on modern religious thought. It is in this sense that Kant is frequently said to be *the* philosopher of modern Christian thought.[18] Of course, it was only after World War II that his suppositions and those of the related schools of historical-critical interpretation were mainstreamed in most denominational seminaries and have now become the prevailing theological perspective in most of the mainline Christian and Jewish communities.

Kant's relativism opened the door to the development in Germany of the philosophy of nihilism developed by Friedrich Nietzsche (1844–1900) and the relativism of the sociologist Max Weber (1864–1920). In addition, the Kantian "turn to the subject" made possible the emergence of psychology and Sigmund Freud's approach to it. Likewise, the widespread endorsement of Kant led to the introduction in America—and now the general appropriation by the public—of nihilism (and its narcissist tendencies), along with a therapeutic orientation. The thoroughness of the infiltration of their ideas in the American social psyche is evidenced by the frequency in American slang of terms such as "values" (implying that we choose our own sense of the good), "free spirit," and "healthy ego," along with admonitions not to "lose yourself in love" or to practice the "Protestant work ethic."[19]

It needs to be emphasized that these phrases, as well as their intellectual antecedents, presuppose an anti-Augustinian, optimistic view of human persons. Each presupposes that people know what is good for them and are capable of achieving their aims, especially if no one and nothing gets in their way.

The preceding analysis is not intended to suggest that the trends of the academy in the second half of the twentieth century are the sole factor in the emergence of narcissism and the therapeutic ethos of our day. We have observed the impact of media and economic dynamics in making this happen, not to mention our innate concupiscent desires. However, the impact of American universities on the American social ethos from the mid-1940s through the 1960s is evident. Today's opinion makers and their values were shaped by the German Enlightenment views that dominated on the college campuses of their day, and these alumni brought these ways of looking at the world with them in the grown-up world they now control.

Insofar as the relativism of Kant and his heirs that has come to dominate the academy is now in the popular social air we breathe, locating all that is good in what the individual determines is good, the American university is not so elitist after all. Indeed, at least in the humanities and social sciences, it is not standing for much more than the therapeutic ethos and social narcissism that dominate American society today, albeit in a more abstract, less titillating way. In its present state the American university will not make much of an impact, at least not until it begins to recover a constitutional Augustinian orientation in its curriculum and its overall ethos.

With reference to the inability of the academy to criticize trends in society, the very ethos of the American university illustrates the degree to which the latest therapeutic trends in society are endorsed and even emphasized on college campuses. For example, at Colby College (in Waterville, Maine) no speech may undermine self-esteem. Everywhere on America's campuses inclusive language is mandated. In many scholarly circles of the humanities, it is a basic supposition that the ideology of oppressed groups should furnish the framework for all investigations of history (for we can never be objective). Sexual harassment is the great taboo. Penn State opposed all topics raised in class that are experienced as harassment. Another concern is "nontraditional violence," which is perpetrated when someone and his or her views are criticized. Criticism is bad manners in many intellectually elite circles. As a result, when criticism does emerge there are no social norms, so it is often done in bad taste as an attack on the person of the scholar, not on the ideas articulated.

We have noted in previous chapters that sensitivity to minorities, equal rights, affirmation of the cultural heritage of minorities, and even measures to balance power and privileges so that these social goods are shared more equally with the oppressed are important constitutional values.[20] The problem in these characteristic examples of contemporary college life is that there is no due process. The community is judging not what constitutes harassment, but feelings. The dominance of the therapeutic outlook is evident. There are good intentions behind these developments: the concern to protect minorities. The problem is that the Constitution's vision of human beings as self-interested, so that truth can emerge only in dialogue, has been forfeited.

In place of this vision have emerged two options with similar individualistic presuppositions, which for that reason cannot be brought into dialogue. One segment of the academy holds to an Enlightenment optimism about human nature, which presupposes that there may be some viewpoints that are not marred by a self-interested agenda (especially the agenda of minorities). The other, often termed deconstruction, and frequently marketed as multiculturalism, assumes a more radical postmodernist version of the Enlightenment agenda, radicalizing Kantian perspectivalism. Thus its proponents totally reject the possibility of absolute truth emerging in dialogue, because everything is ultimately relative. For this segment of academia, standards and claims to truth have been deemed intimately related to the exercise of political muscle. Consequently, these scholars often assert that the classics of Western culture do not speak to minorities, since these works (or at least their standard interpretations) are in the interests of preserving the social power of White males.[21] Given these options, there is no longer much real dialogue on many university campuses. Proponents of the prevailing options talk past each other.

There is not much room for intellectual risk and challenge in this environment. The easiest way to go is to accept the propaganda expounded by one's instructors (to give the professors what they want). The outcome is that students either get radicalized in this way (mostly on the surface) or reject the value-relativism that dominates on campus and simply experience college as a credentialing process that has no value to them except as a ticket to a "good" job.[22]

This last point, the impact of the business ethos on our college campuses and their intellectual life, the degree to which the university is effectively forfeiting its ability to function as a countercultural force, surfaces in other ways. The business paradigm is reflected on college campuses in that corporate funding has pressured universities and liberal arts colleges to beef up science, math, and business departments, and more recently to create computer science departments. By contrast, liberal arts departments have less and less clout, as comparatively they receive less and less funding. No less evident is the way university administrators operate. The prevailing business model of team management has taken root on American campuses. Very rarely does the president or the dean operate by fiat, as in former times (especially in church-related institutions). But that does not mean that decisions about curriculum and personnel matters such as tenure are determined by open debate. Instead, they are managed through faculty committees.[23]

It is certainly apparent that by most of the avant-garde standards of contemporary culture, the American university and its correlated professional schools have become "politically correct," right down to the fact that today one can receive credit for classes in contemporary culture analyzing television, gender studies, and Black film, as well as by participating in service learning reflection. In so doing, though, they have lost a certain rapport they once had with the Middle America when intellectual life was respected and influential. American higher education is also forfeiting its countercultural status and ability to influence change.

Where Does Common Sense Lead Our Schools?

It is evident that as much as in the case of any of the social problems examined in this book, our schools have been hurt by the silencing of the Augustinian-constitutional perspective in favor of the optimism of the German Enlightenment. The emphasis on the essential goodness of human beings leads to intellectual commitments and educational practices that presume that individuals always want to learn, are innately creative, and know what is best for them and their children. Obviously, these suppositions and the educational strategies they have influenced do not work.

What would restoring the viability of an Augustinian-constitutional viewpoint in our schools and in society in general do for our educational system? At the most rudimentary level, it would provide another life option, a way of interpreting reality that differs from the prevailing Enlightenment optimism and its relativistic intellectual heirs. The educational process always wins when students are exposed to a variety of perspectives, to new ways of thinking (even if these "new" ways are actually quite old).

Reincarnating the Augustinian view would also make us more humble about our schools and about social life in general. Those who know of their sinfulness or that self-interest makes them tick are more likely aware that their thinking is selfish, not always in interests of the greater or common good. Such persons are also aware that tied in with their selfishness is a bit of sloth or desire to find the easy way, to be blown by the winds of change, and to sacrifice the future for instant gratification.

With a restoration of this sort of Augustinian way of thinking in place in American society, perhaps more parents would realize that because they do not have all the answers, they must continue to set aside egocentricity and be comfortable taking guidance from authority figures such as teachers. Of course, concupiscent teachers and administrators aware of their fallenness also recognize that they do not have all the answers. They too need the dialogue with parents and the public in general about dealing with the kids and with curricular matters. But seeing the mutual need that all these authorities have of one another could lead to the formation of the sort of united front required by shared authority for the authority to function well. Just as parents had better agree in public about how they raise their kids (or the children will divide and conquer), so standards will never be restored in public education if children do not perceive parents, teachers, and administrators as on the same page.

This constitutional perspective, which brings the realization that an interplay of all the factions is required to make the system work efficiently, is one that American higher education needs to reappropriate. Until it does, our colleges will continue to fail to be places of genuine public debate and will fail to provide an integrated education rather than the present grab-bag of dipping into one specialization after another.

One more related Augustinian contribution to our educational system deserves our attention. Suppose our schools began to embrace the realism of this worldview, took seriously that the creativity of students (both children and adults) is likely to emerge, like most social values, only with a certain degree of coercion (through high standards that are really enforced). I believe that educational results might improve significantly. Our natural sloth and propensity to be swayed by irregular passions or by the latest or strongest representation offered by society's authorities (Madison) means that unless students are coerced by high standards to really enter "worlds" other than their own, there will be no growth, no real education.[24]

Augustinian Common Sense

The High Costs of Its Neglect

This whole book has offered an extended commentary on the costs of our neglecting Augustinian and constitutional common sense. We have observed how this neglect has been occasioned by at least three distinct, though related, movements that have made their presence felt in America since World War II: (1) the impact of the ideas of the German Enlightenment on American popular culture; (2) new post-1960s business trends (especially the commitment of American business to flexibility and customizing products, which has, since the Reagan years, led to increased social power and influence as the influence of organized labor wanes); and (3) the widespread dissemination of new technologies (especially television and the computer). As a result, an optimistic view of human nature has become the generally accepted presupposition for modern American thinking. This optimism, derived at least indirectly from German Enlightenment intellectuals (chiefly Kant, Nietzsche, and Weber, as well as popularized versions of Freud), has had serious costs.

I reiterate how much support there is for my conclusions. Perhaps the most convincing was the previously mentioned *New York Times* survey that revealed that 73 percent of Americans believed that people are born good and that 85 percent believed they could be pretty much anything they wanted to be.[1]

181

Because many Americans have come to believe that they are essentially good and that the problems in life and society are caused by others, it is politically correct to affirm oneself and one's perceptions of reality. Unhealthy behavior is thought to be occasioned by the subordination of one's needs and wants to someone else or to some greater social good. Such glorification of oneself leads to individualism, to relativism (for only my perceptions count for me), and even to narcissism (for others are there only to meet my needs). This sort of existence leads to loneliness, to the perception that ultimately we do not share much in common. Thus, belief in common values gradually ebbs with this optimistic view of human nature. Even if relativism is not posited, in the final analysis I do not need my neighbor, because I know the good through reason or intuition. Ultimately, I am alone.

Solitary individuals are vulnerable. The power of the establishment can more readily have its way with them. They are more readily blown by the winds of change, especially as the media and other opinion makers would manipulate them. It takes social organization to protect us from the powers that be and from ourselves, and solitary individuals tend to be more unhappy. This point was made in polls completed for the DDB Needham Life Style Survey in 1998 and 1999. The surveys found that those Americans with some social connections (through churches, clubs, and other organizations) characterize themselves at a level of happiness above the national average. Presumably on a statistical basis, then, one can conclude that those who experience loneliness have levels of happiness below the national average, and so are less happy than those engaged in community. This observation seems confirmed insofar as the surveys also noted a decline since 1975 in the national average of those who consider themselves happy. Insofar as there has been less engagement in community activities and more Americans living in solitude, as witnessed by that marked increase in never-married adults ages 30 to 34 (from 6 percent to 22 percent), we must conclude that there is a relationship between the lowered levels of happiness and the increased solitude Americans experience.[2]

We have noted how the solitude that has resulted from the optimistic view of human nature that Americans have adopted has contributed to a relativizing of values and religious commitments, and to a preoccupation with finding self-gratification and self-fulfillment, culminating in a cult of celebrity and a social narcissism that reduces human beings to mere things whose only function is to serve the ego. The emergence of the therapeutic ethos of contemporary American culture, as well as its present preoccupation with business and its mad chase for wealth, has both resulted from these dynamics and fed them. The data provided in this book have suggested that when preoccupation with self-fulfillment and a sense that all values are relative to the subject become the dominant passion and the prevailing worldview, the result is not good for society or for the individual.

We have noted the negative social consequences of this preoccupation with the individual emerging from a belief that individuals are essentially good. Our celebration of the free market and push for small government follow from the contention that people and the economic system are good and fair, that success is always merited. As a result, the economic disparities between Whites and racial minorities, between males and females, remain. The rich get richer, the poor get poorer, and the safety net for the poor and the elderly shrinks more and more. Standards of morality and those of the educational system continue to be lowered as we blissfully assume the goodness of human nature (at least our own goodness and those of our closest associates). Respect for institutions and their authority withers, as long as we continue to think of ourselves as self-sufficient and capable of getting along without them. And as these institutions become more distant and wither, we become more isolated and less content. The list goes on and on.

My appeal to revivify the constitutional vision of human nature, the Augustinian view of original sin, among the American public entails several paradoxical points. The realism—even cynicism—about human nature and its institutions paradoxically leads to a sense of the individual's need and appreciation for these institutions and the people who constitute them. In a sense, this is a function of the paradoxical character of the Augustinian view (as well as its constitutional embodiment).

The Augustinian view of human nature's full appropriation paradoxically can counteract present American cynicism about government and other institutions. This constitutional vision reminds us that we need to be just as suspicious of ourselves and our motives as of others and their motives. What we as individuals want in society is not likely what is best for us and certainly not what is good for society as a whole. Only in dialogue, in the push-pull, bickering tradeoffs of politicking (conducted with fair rules) can we find something approaching fairness.

Again paradoxically, the affirmation of the realism and cynicism of Augustinian and constitutional thinking is not to deny a place for affirming the goodness of humanity. Christians have always asserted that the first and last word about humanity is not sinfulness, but that it was created good (Gen. 1:31). The framer of the doctrine of original sin also affirmed, as America's founders did, that we can know what the good is. Like them, he posited a natural law accessible to reason as the criterion for all sociopolitical judgments.[3] Augustine proceeded even more profoundly in affirming humanity's goodness, contending that our goodness is enhanced by our relation to the creation as a whole.[4] In that sense he affirms what I have contended in this book, that human life gets even better when we recognize the need for interrelationships and cooperation with each other. The classical Christian tradition has always contended that an affirmation of human sinfulness must be made in paradoxical tension with an awareness of human goodness.

The same paradox is evident, as we have seen, in the constitutional heritage. Side-by-side with the Augustinian strand is the more optimistic strand derived primarily from John Locke's confidence in humanity's ability to know and to do the good.[5] These two strands belong together. Affirming only the Augustinian perspective apart from the distinct Judeo-Christian affirmations of the goodness of creation or the concept of the natural law, we would run the risk of creating social policies without sufficient concern for human rights. And just as the Constitution makes this affirmation of human goodness and worth not by appeal to distinct Christian teaching but by appeal to the Enlightenment's vision, so this Enlightenment strand of thought has validity for Americans (even American Christians). It is useful in enabling the affirmation of the good of which people are capable as a check against unhealthy cynicism and defeatism, which might emerge should the Augustinian view of reality stand alone.

It is true that I have sought in this book to emphasize the Augustinian strand. But I have done so only because the more optimistic viewpoint has become almost monolithic in much of contemporary society, to the point of its being the American social system's distortion. The genius of the constitutional system may be that it holds these two truths together in paradoxical tension. And as noted, the paradoxical affirmation of both strands is not inimical to Christian faith.

Another reason for highlighting how these two strands of constitutional thinking belong together is to prevent my appeal for reviving Augustinian common sense from being taken as Christian exclusivism, effectively disenfranchising Jews, Muslims, secular humanists, and other non-Christians. To be sure, these Americans do not endorse with Christians the doctrine of original sin. They might, however (and I would encourage them to), endorse the concept of humans as self-interested, even selfish or concupiscent. Proponents of these traditions might not be inclined to regard these characteristics as necessarily negative. Certainly it would be compatible with these traditions to deem self-interest and selfishness as neutral, as characteristics that are capable of distortion and that therefore must be counterbalanced. From my perspective, though, Christians are more in touch with the Constitution at this point, as they have a more heightened awareness than other citizens of the mischief human beings can cause. Consequently, American Christians are best situated to be prophetic voices for justice. That is not surprising, given the Christian influences we have identified in the Constitution.

Is Augustinian Common Sense a Lost Cause?

The restoration of an Augustinian vision, though the call to it is presently out of fashion in the higher echelons of American society, is not an impossible task. Paradoxically, in a sense it is nothing more than a return to roots (the grass roots).

The optimistic view of Enlightenment thinking was never a movement of the masses, but one of the elite. After all, the Enlightenment, particularly its Lockean and German versions, first saw the light of day in the universities, and we should recall that at least its German variety rooted in Kant's philosophy did not really filter down to the masses until after World War II.[6]

By contrast, the Augustinian vision has been a "popular" philosophy of the masses in at least two senses. Most obviously, its Christian character expressed the thinking of most Americans, who at least until recently were practicing Christians. Also, the American version of Augustine, if not the African Father's own views, ran counter to the relativism of German Enlightenment thinking, which would lead us to think that ultimately we are alone and share little in common, not even our own values.

Recall that the American appropriation of Augustine's thought was largely mediated through the philosophy of Scottish Common Sense Realism. And the Scottish philosophers maintained the belief that it is possible to establish normative common-sense meaning in a community and, correspondingly, that we can discern objective moral truth, which is really just common sense.[7]

This appeal to common sense as the basis for a community, socially accepted truth is almost premodern in character (the way most people thought prior to the Enlightenment). Until the German Enlightenment strands we have considered in this book began to make their impact on American life after the 1950s, the belief that absolute truth can be obtained dominated in American life. It was and continued to be the viewpoint of the masses.

Recent survey data demonstrate that relativism has not completely overtaken this early American Augustinian confidence in obtaining absolute truth. As recently as 1991 a survey conducted by Barna Research Group indicated that one-third of the American public believed in absolute truth. In January 2000 that figure went as high as 38 percent pertaining to absolute moral truth, dropping to 22 percent in November 2001.[8]

Another set of statistics is relevant, though perhaps more ambiguously so, for making the case that Americans have not yet completely forfeited the Augustinian paradigm's insistence that human beings need community to safeguard themselves from themselves. A 1991 study by eminent American sociologist Robert Wuthnow indicated that 80 million Americans were involved in volunteer activity. In a 1994 study he reports that fully 40 percent of all Americans claim to be involved in a small group that meets regularly. Interestingly, the acclaimed political scientist Robert Putnam contends that there are even higher levels of voluntarism among Generation X than among the youngest of the Baby Boomers.[9]

It is evident, then, that a reappropriation of the Augustinian viewpoint has a lot of residual resonance in the public. There is not only a core of nay-sayers to the extreme relativism and even to the individualism associated with the German Enlightenment. According to the previously cited *New York Times* poll, at least nearly 30 percent of the public do not believe that we are born good, and more of those who do not currently see it that way are churchgoers who are a logical target audience for instruction in the churches toward a new constitutional appreciation. Augustinian common sense is not dead. It just needs more advocates like readers of this book to help it make inroads with the elite.

Like most things essentially Christian, the Augustinian view of original sin is paradoxical, not correctly deployed if not held in tension with its opposite pole. Life itself is full of such paradoxes, as life and death often go together, as youth and maturity relate, as male and female relate. The great documents of human life, such as the Bible and the U.S. Constitution, have been found to be classics precisely because they have been able to express this paradoxical character of life.

In addition to the paradoxes associated with the Augustinian-constitutional vision that we have noted, there is an ultimate paradox it embodies. This relates to the behavioral outcomes, noted in the conclusion of the first chapter, that its widespread reappropriation might enhance. It seems that Americans can become people who care a lot more for each other to the degree that they begin to recognize that they are not essentially good, but are really selfish. Vigilance about the low sides of human nature, a healthy cynicism, improves civic life.

Notes

Introduction

1. For references to Niebuhr, see chapter 1, nn. 31 and 33. For these commitments in the views of Martin Luther King Jr., see his "Pilgrimage to Nonviolence," in James M. Washington, ed., *A Testament of Hope: The Essential Writings of Martin Luther King, Jr.* (San Francisco: Harper & Row, 1986), 35–36; and "I Have a Dream" (1963) in the same collection, 217–18. For other publications in this tradition, see James H. Smylie, "Madison and Witherspoon: Theological Roots of American Political Thought," *Princeton University Library Chronicle* 22 (1960–61): 118–32; Jean Bethke Elshtain, *Augustine and the Limits of Politics* (Notre Dame, Ind.: University of Notre Dame Press, 1995); and Ronald William Dworkin, *The Rise of the Imperial Self: America's Culture Wars in Augustinian Perspective* (Lanham, Md.: Rowan & Littlefield, 1996).

2. From 1970 to 1997, the proportion of American households making above $75,000 per year more than doubled (from 9 percent of American families in 1970 to 18.4 percent in 1997). But while there has been a decrease in the number of those making under $10,000 annually, those families making only $10,000 to $14,000 increased from 7.5 percent in 1970 to 8.1 percent in 1997. Likewise, the *Congressional Quarterly Researcher* (Jan.–Dec. 1999): 1004–1005, noted that from 1992 to1998 the American economy averaged an annual growth of 3.6 percent, while wages of the average worker grew only 3 percent annually. The average annual increase in consumer spending in this period was 5.3 percent, nearly double the increase in wages. The obvious conclusion is that it costs more to maintain a certain lifestyle, and that the middle class has been losing ground in the midst of the overall prosperity.

3. A January 2001 Gallup poll indicates that 44 percent of the middle class were anxious about the future (*Gallup Poll Monthly*, no. 425 [Feb. 2001], 27). For a detailed discussion of the personality characteristics stimulated by the new economy, see Richard Sennett, *The Corrosion of Character: The Personal Consequences of Work in the New Capitalism* (New York and London: W. W. Norton & Company, 1998).

4. Christopher Lasch, *The Culture of Narcissism: American Life in an Age of Diminishing Expectations* (New York: W. W. Norton & Company, 1979); John Miller, *Egotopia* (Mobile: University of Alabama Press, 1997).

5. See chap. 1, nn. 10–11 and chap. 2, n. 28 for references to Augustine's and Madison's views. The thesis that the Constitution is shaped by the doctrine of original sin has been affirmed by Page Smith, *The Constitution: A Documentary and Narrative History* (New York: Morrow Quill, 1980), esp. 414. The relativism in Western thought is indebted to the distinction made by Immanuel Kant (*Critique of Pure Reason*, trans. Norman Kemp Smith [Toronto: Macmillan, 1929], 257ff.) between the noumenon (the

thing-in-itself) and the phenomenon (one's perception of the noumenon). Given these suppositions, relativism is inevitable, because the real content of knowledge is not objective data, but the thought processes of the individual in perceiving noumena. For penetrating comments about the way in which relativism has permeated contemporary American society, see Allan Bloom, *The Closing of the American Mind* (New York: Simon and Schuster, 1987), esp. 25–26.

6. For evidences of Freud's cynical realism about human nature, see his *Civilization and Its Discontents*, trans. James Strachey (New York: W. W. Norton, 1961), 30, 89–90. For a similar assessment that Jung's optimistic adaptation of Freud has had greater impact on modern psychology than Freud's own realism, see Calvin Hall and Gardner Lindzey, *Theories of Personality*, 2d ed. (New York and London: John Wiley & Sons, 1970), 111–12.

7. For more descriptions of this ethos, see Wendy Kaminer, *I'm Dysfunctional, You're Dysfunctional: The Recovery Movement and Other Self-Help Fashions* (Redding, Mass.: Addison-Wesley, 1992); and Charles J. Sykes, *A Nation of Victims: The Decay of the American Character* (New York: St. Martin's, 1992).

8. Bloom, *Closing*, 148ff.

9. For a fuller analysis of narcissism, see Lasch, *Culture of Narcissism*, esp. 80ff.

10. U.S. Bureau of the Census, *Statistical Abstract of the United States: 2000*, (Washington, D.C.: USGPO, 2000), 475.

11. For this analysis of the dynamics of contemporary marketing, see Lasch, *Culture of Narcissism*, 137–38. See also Rodney Clapp, ed., *The Consuming Passion: Christianity and the Culture of Consumption* (Downers Grove, Ill.: InterVarsity Press, 1987).

12. For these observations, I am indebted to Paul H. Nystrom, *Economics of Fashion* (New York: Ronald Press, 1928), 67–68.

13. *Congressional Quarterly Researcher* (Jan.–Dec. 1999): 1004.

14. *Gallup Poll Monthly*, no. 387 (Dec. 1997): 48–49.

15. For this analysis, I am indebted to William Ophuls, *Requiem for Modern Politics: The Tragedy of the Enlightenment and the Challenge of the New Millennium* (Boulder, Colo.: Westview Press, 1997), 79–82.

16. These statistics were reported by Genevieve Wood, the vice president of the Family Research Council, on CNN's *Crossfire*, 9 May 2002.

17. For these insights, I am indebted to Ivan Illich. Also see Jacques Ellul, *The Technological Society* (London: Cape, 1964); cf. Søren Kierkegaard, *Either/Or*, trans. Walter Lowrie, 2 vols. (Princeton: Princeton University Press, 1944), 2:5ff.

18. Robert Reich (*The Work of Nations* [New York: Vintage, 1992]) was not the first to articulate this theme, but his own work, particularly when view" ed as a paradigm for attitudes in the Clinton administration in which he served, did much to popularize the idea of a meritocracy. For a discussion of the thoroughgoing dominance of this ideology in the powers that be, see Christopher Lasch, *The Revolt of the Elites and the Betrayal of Democracy* (New York and London: W. W. Norton & Company, 1995), 39–44; cf. Michael Young, *The Rise of the Meritocracy, 1870–2033* (New York: Transaction, 1999).

19. For these insights, I am indebted to Lawrence M. Friedman, *The Horizontal Society* (New Haven: Yale University Press, 1999), 75–76. See also Barbara Ehrenreich, *The Fear of Falling: The Inner Life of the Middle Class* (New York: Pantheon, 1987).

20. For these observations, I am indebted to Lasch, *Revolt of the Elites*, esp. 44.

21. See William F. May, *Beleaguered Rulers: The Public Obligation of the Professional* (Louisville: Westminster Press, 2001). These dynamics seem related to the public's decreased appreciation of these professions.

22. Lasch, *Revolt of the Elites*, 124–27.

23. U.S. Census Bureau, *Statistical Abstract of the United States: 2000*, 211.

24. *Congressional Quarterly Researcher* (Jan.–Dec. 1999): 1004–1005; Sharon Epperson, "Make No (Big) Mistake," *Time*, 23 July 2000, 73; Gregory Zuckerman, "U.S. Boom: Living on Borrowed Dime?" *Wall Street Journal*, 31 Dec. 1999; Yochi J. Dreazen, "Rate at Which Consumers Save Sinks to a Record," *Wall Street Journal*, 1 February 2000.

25. *New York Times Magazine*, 7 May 2000; also reported in Alan Wolfe, *Moral Freedom: The Search for Virtue in a World of Choice* (New York and London: W. W. Norton & Company, 2001), 169, 197.

26. This characterization of the heart of the Enlightenment has been offered by Karl Barth, *Church Dogmatics* IV/1, ed. G. W. Bromiley and T. F. Torrance (Edinburgh: T&T Clark, 1956), 479. For examples of the optimistic view of human nature of certain key Enlightenment figures, see John Toland, *Christianity Not Mysterious* (1696); John Locke, *The Reasonableness of Christianity* (1731), 231; Gotthold Lessing, *The Education of the Human Race* (1780), esp. 4; and Immanuel Kant, *Religion within the Limits of Reason Alone* (1793), vol. 1, pt. 4 .

Chapter 1

1. Anthony, in *The Sayings of the Desert Fathers*, 1, 3, 33.

2. Matoes, Longinus, and Moses the Negro in *Sayings of the Desert Fathers*, pp. 2,7,9; 2–4; and 5 respectively; *The Instructions of Commodianus* (240), 64.

3. Athanasius, *On the Incarnation of the Word* (316–318), 5–7, 13–14, 54.

4. Tertullian, *On Exhortation to Chastity* (n.d.), II; Cyprian of Carthage, *Epistles* (n.d.), 64/58.5.

5. Pelagius, *Letter to Demetriaden* (n.d.), 16; Augustine, *The Confessions* (397), 10.29.40.

6. Augustine, *Confessions*, 1.5.5ff., 10.28.39.

7. Augustine, *On the Spirit and the Letter* (412), 5.

8. This viewpoint is not inconsistent with Augustine's claim that free will is not denied by asserting grace, that there is a cooperation of grace and works in bringing about salvation, a view articulated in his *On Grace and Free Will* (426/427), 1,43. But I am not sure it is in fact what he states. See Augustine, *A Treatise on Nature and Grace, against Pelagius* (415), 46.54. The Lutheran church's Augsburg Confession (1530), XVIII, does expressly maintain that we have freedom in ordinary daily decisions while, without grace, ever remaining in bondage to sin.

9. Augustine, *Confessions*, 6.12.22, 6.15.25; 13.7.8; Augustine, *City of God* (413–426), 14.15.

10. Augustine, *On Marriage and Concupiscence* (419/420), 1.21.24–22.25; cf. Augustine, *To Simplician—On Various Questions* (395/396), 2.20.

11. Augustine, *To Simplician*, 2.10

12. Augustine, *Ten Homilies on the Epistle of John to the Parthians* (ca. 417), 8.9.

13. Augustine, *A Treatise against Two Letters of the Pelagians* (420), III.20–21; cf. Martin Luther, *Commentary on Psalm 51* (1532), in Jaroslav Pelikan, ed., *Luther's Works*, vol. 12 (St. Louis: Concordia Publishing House, 1955), 400–1; *Apology of the Augsburg Confession* (1531), XVIII.9.

14. Augustine, *On Grace and Free Will,* 8.

15. Augustine, *On Christian Doctrine* (397), 1.22.20–21; 1.33.36.

16. For a more detailed early sketch of this vision of eternal life, see Mark Ellingsen, *A Common Sense Theology: The Bible, Faith, and American Society* (Macon, Ga.: Mercer University Press, 1995), 203–204.

17. There is an increasing openness in the scientific community to the belief that human life began with a common African mother. See Allan C. Wilson and Rebecca L. Cann, "The Recent African Genesis of Humans," *Scientific American* (April 1992): 69–71; Christopher Stringer and Robin McKie, *African Exodus: The Origins of Modern Humanity* (New York: Henry Holt, 1997).

18. Augustine, *On Marriage and Concupiscence* (419–420), 1.24.27; 2.14.29; Augustine, *On Original Sin* (418), 2.33.38; Augustine, *On Rebuke and Grace* (426/427), 13.42; cf. Cyprian of Carthage, *Epistles,* 64/58.5.

19. Barth, *Church Dogmatics* IV/1, esp. 492. It should be noted that Barth himself did not elaborate much on how interaction with other concupiscent beings shapes the sinner's being. In fact, it might be possible to accuse him of reducing the sinful condition to sinful actions. But see p. 507 for a mitigating qualification that may exonerate him from that charge.

20. Augustine, *On Marriage and Concupiscence,* 23.25.

21. Augustine, *The City of God,* 19.5.

22. Ibid., 14.28.

23. The Lutheran *Apology of the Augsburg Confession,* II.23–24; John Calvin, *Institutes of the Christian Religion* (1562), 2.1.8; 3.3.10. Martin Luther made a point very much like this equation of sin with concupiscence when he described the sinful condition as being "turned in on oneself" (*Lectures on Romans* [1515–17], in Hilton C. Oswald, ed., *Luther's Works,* 55 vols. [Philadelphia: Fortress, 1972], 25:345).

24. Augustine, *On Marriage and Concupiscence,* 1.23.25.

25. On the Puritan paradigm, see Sydney E. Ahlstrom, *A Religious History of the American People* (New Haven: Yale University Press, 1972), esp. 3, 12, 1079, 1094–96; and Mark Ellingsen, *Reclaiming Our Roots: An Inclusive Introduction to Church History,* 2 vols. (Harrisburg, Pa.: Trinity, 1999), esp. 2:198ff. Insofar as the key theological categories he employed for interpreting American Christianity were Calvinist/Puritan in character, we might consider in support of this analysis H. Richard Niebuhr, *The Kingdom of God in America* (New York: Harper & Row, 1937). Regarding the impact of the Westminster Confession on American Puritanism, it should be noted that adherence to its doctrines was attested as early as 1648 at the Cambridge Synod of New England Puritans, and subsequently ratified in other meetings in 1680 and 1708.

26. For Augustinian commitments in Methodism, Lutheranism, Catholicism, and Pentecostalism, see the [Methodist] Articles of Religion (n.d.), 7; the Augsburg Confession, II; Catechism of the Catholic Church (1992), 416–19; and Church of God in Christ, *Official Manual* (1973), 54–55.

27. Thomas Reid, *Essays on the Active Powers of Man,* in *The Works of Thomas Reid,* vol. 2, 7th ed. (Edinburgh: Maclachlan and Stewart, 1872), 585.

28. Francis Hutcheson, *An Essay on the Nature and Conduct of the Passions and Affections with Illustrations on the Moral Sense* (1742), 3d ed. (Gainesville, Fla.: Scholars' Facsimiles & Reprints, 1969), 32–34, 193, 236–37; and Francis Hutcheson, *An Inquiry into the Original of Our Ideas of Beauty and Virtue* (1725) (New York: Garland, 1971), 115–16, 173 ff. Also see Garry Wills, *Inventing America: Jefferson's Declaration of Independence* (New York: Vintage, 1979), 288–89; and Knud Haakonssen, "Intro-

duction," in Thomas Reid, *Practical Ethics*, ed. Knud Haakonssen (Princeton: Princeton University Press, 1990), 53–56. The latter text provides a helpful discussion of the differences between Hutcheson and Reid. For Reid's rejection of Hutcheson's emphasis on self-interest, see Reid, *Essays on the Active Powers of Man*, 2:650, 584–92.

29. John Witherspoon, *The Works of John Witherspoon*, 9 vols. (Edinburgh: Ogle & Aikman, 1805), 9:139.

30. Jack Scott, ed., *An Annotated Edition of Lectures on Moral Philosophy* (Newark: University of Delaware Press, 1982), 144.

31. Reinhold Niebuhr, "Law, Conscience, and Grace," in *Justice and Mercy*, ed. Ursula M. Niebuhr (repr., Louisville: Westminster/John Knox Press, 1991), 43.

32. Ibid., 44.

33. Reinhold Niebuhr, *Nature and Destiny of Man: A Christian Interpretation*, 2 vols. (New York: Charles Scribner's Sons, 1941–43), 2:232.

Chapter 2

1. These two strands have been identified by analysts respectively as the "Classical-Christian Consciousness" (the strand to which the Augustinian, Christian view of human nature obviously belongs) and the "Secular-Democratic Consciousness" (the strand of thought to which the more optimistic view of human nature belongs). See Robert N. Bellah et al., *Habits of the Heart: Individualism and Commitment in American Life* (Berkeley: University of California Press, 1985), esp. 28–35; and Page Smith, *The Constitution: A Documentary and Narrative History* (New York: Morrow Quill, 1980), esp. 336–37, 390, 413–15.

2. James Madison, "Letter to James Madison Sr." (1769), in *The Complete Madison: His Basic Writings*, ed. Saul Padover (New York: Harper & Brothers, 1953), 5. For a fuller discussion of the impact of Common Sense Realism on the elite universities of the colonies, see Sydney E. Ahlstrom, "The Scottish Philosophy and American Theology," *Church History* 24 (1955): 261–65.

3. Thomas Jefferson, *Autobiography* (1821), in Thomas Jefferson, *Writings* (New York: Library of America, 1984), 4; cf. Garry Wills, *Inventing America: Jefferson's Declaration of Independence* (New York: Vintage, 1979), 13–14, 176–80.

4. See Norman S. Fiering, *Moral Philosophy at Seventeenth-Century Harvard: A Discipline in Transition* (Chapel Hill: University of North Carolina Press, 1981), 198–200; Ahlstrom, "Scottish Philosophy," 262–65; Wills, *Inventing America*, 176–77.

5. Thomas Jefferson, "Letter to Dugald Stewart" (1824), in Jefferson, *Writings*, 1488.

6. Thomas Jefferson, "Letter to Robert Skipwith with a List of Books" (1771), in Jefferson, *Writings*, 744.

7. John Dunn, "The Politics of Locke in England and America in the Eighteenth Century," in *John Locke: Problems and Perspectives*, ed. J. W. Yolton (London: Cambridge University Press, 1969), as quoted in Wills, *Inventing America*, 170. Other studies that support this conclusion are also cited by Wills in, *Inventing America*, 170–71.

8. Benjamin Franklin, *Proposals Relating to the Education of Youth in Pennsylvania* (1749), in Benjamin Franklin, *Writings*, ed. J. A. Leo Lemay (New York: Library of America, 1987), 323–24.

9. Thomas Jefferson, "Letter to John Norvell" (1807), in Jefferson, *Writings*, 1176.

10. Thomas Jefferson, "Letter to John Trumbull" (1789), in Jefferson, *Writings*, 939–40.

11. When Jefferson praises Locke for his political insights, the founding father usually links him not with Bacon and Newton (whose contributions were in science and epistemology, not in political theory), but with Algernon Sidney, a seventeenth-century English Whig Party revolutionary and political theorist. See "Minutes of the Board of Visitors, University of Virginia" (1822), in Jefferson, *Writings*, 479; "Letter to Robert Skipwith," in Jefferson, *Writings*, 479 and 744, respectively. In the latter document, it is important to note Jefferson's claim (p. 742) that his concern with books in the field of politics really pertains primarily to what they teach concerning commerce. For an analysis of these texts, see Mark Ellingsen, *A Common Sense Theology: The Bible, Faith, and American Society* (Macon, Ga.: Mercer University Press, 1995), 110; and Wills, *Inventing America*, 170–71.

12. John Locke, *Essay Concerning Human Understanding* (1690), II. ii.2.

13. John Locke, *The Reasonableness of Christianity* (1731), 241.

14. Ibid., 231.

15. John Locke, *Second Treatise on Civil Government* (1690), 4–6, 27, 89, 95ff, 124, 134, 211ff.

16. For some of the influential pamphlets of the era in which Locke was cited as authorization in an appeal for the patriots' natural rights, see James Otis, *Rights of the British Colonies Asserted and Proved* (Boston: JHL Pamphlet 7, 1764:), 9, 15, 22–23, 25, 26, 27, 30, 37; James Otis, *A Vindication of the British Colonies . . .* (Boston, JHL Pamphlet 11,1765:), 10–12; Alexander Hamilton, *The Farmer Refuted . . .* (New York, 1755), in Harold C. Syrett et al., ed, *The Papers of Alexander Hamilton*, 27 vols. (New York: Columbia University Press, 1961–1987), 1:86.

17. David Hume, *On the Independency of Parliament (1741–1742)*, in David Hume, *The Philosphical Works*, 4 vols., ed. Thomas Hill Green and Thomas Hodge Grose, (London, 1886), 3:117–18. For Hume's epistemology, see his *Enquiry concerning Human Understanding* (1758/1777), IV.I; XII.I.

18. Baron de Montesquieu, *Spirit of the Laws* (1748). See David A. J. Richards, *Foundations of American Constitutionalism* (New York and Oxford: Oxford University Press, 1989), 122–23, 127–29; and Forrest McDonald, *Novus Ordo Seculorum: The Intellectual Origins of the Constitution* (Lawrence: University of Kansas, 1985), 80–83, 199–200, 233–35. Some historians believe that the founders may also have been influenced by Machiavelli, who not unlike Augustine, endorsed a pessimistic view of persons. See his *The Prince* (1513), XVIII; Richards, *Foundations*, 147, 287, 289, 295; and McDonald, *Novus Ordo*, 70. William Ophuls (*Requiem for Modern Politics* [Boulder, Colo.: Westview Press, 1997], 34), has argued for the impact of Thomas Hobbes on Madison and other founders. Also see Frank M. Coleman, *Hobbes and America* (Toronto: University of Toronto Press, 1977). Hobbes's belief that passion and desire dominate human beings (*Leviathan* [1642], VI) is clearly in line with the Augustinian views of the founders. However, it is noteworthy that the founders do not cite Hobbes in this connection. Nor do they share his and Machiavelli's total moral skepticism, as for Hobbes society is *simply* about preserving public order (*Leviathan*, VIII). But as we will note, the founders affirmed certain objective moral principles rooted in the natural law. See Richards, *Foundations*, 49–51.

19. Benjamin Franklin, "Letter to David Hume" (1760), in Benjamin Franklin, *Writings*, 776. Also see his "Letter to David Hume" (1762), in *Writings*, 786–88.

20. Thomas Jefferson, "Letter to William Duane" (1810), in Jefferson, *Writings*, 1227–31; Thomas Jefferson, "Letter to François D'Ivernois" (1795), in Jefferson, *Writings*, 1024.

21. Thomas Jefferson, "Letter to A. L. C. Destutt de Tracy" (1811), in Jefferson, *Writings*, 1242–43.

22. *Notes of Debates in the Federal Convention of 1787, Reported by James Madison* (New York: Norton, 1987), 311.

23. Thomas Jefferson, "Letter to William Green Munford" (1799), in Jefferson, *Writings*, 1064–66.

24. Thomas Jefferson, "Notes on the State of Virginia" (1782), in Jefferson, *Writings*, 246; Thomas Jefferson, in *Debates in the Several State Conventions on the Adoption of the Federal Constitution*, ed. Jonathan Elliot, 5 vols. (Philadelphia: J.B. Lippincott, 1836), 2:536–37; James Madison, "No. 57," *The Federalist Papers* (New York: Mentor, 1961), 350–51; James Madison, "No. 62," *The Federalist Papers*, 376.

25. James Bryce, as quoted in H. Richard Niebuhr, *The Kingdom of God in America* (repr., New York: Harper, 1959), 79. In support of the thesis that Madison and the American system are dependent on the Augustinian view of human nature of Witherspoon, see James Smylie, "Madison and Witherspoon: Theological Roots of American Thought," *Princeton University Library Chronicle* 22 (Spring 1961): 118–32; and L. Gordon Tait, *The Piety of John Witherspoon: Pew, Pulpit, and Public Forum* (Louisville: Geneva, 2001), esp. 44–45.

26. *Notes of Debates*, 34, 52, 131, 233–34, 311–12, 322–23.

27. Benjamin Franklin, "The Busy-Body, No. 4," *Writings*, 98.

28. James Madison, "No. 10" and "No. 51," *The Federalist Papers*, 77–84, 324–25.

29. *Notes of Debates*, 3.

30. James Madison, "No. 55," *The Federalist Papers*, p346. For analysis of the way in which this text has been used by some critics of the impact of original sin on Madison, and for a way to respond to these critics, I am indebted to Smylie, "Madison and Witherspoon," 128–29.

31. James Madison, "No. 49," *The Federalist Papers*, 314–15.

32. James Madison, "No. 51," *The Federalist Papers*, 323.

33. James Madison, "No. 63," *The Federalist Papers*, 384.

34. Alexander Hamilton, "No. 71," *The Federalist Papers*, 432.

35. Alexander Hamilton, "No. 29," *The Federalist Papers*, 186; Alexander Hamilton, "No. 31", *The Federalist Papers*, 193, 194; Alexander Hamilton, "No. 75," *The Federalist Papers*, 448; Alexander Hamilton, "No. 84," *The Federalist Papers*, 517; Alexander Hamilton, "No. 85," *The Federalist Papers*, 523.

36. James Madison, "No. 51," *The Federalist Papers*, 324–25.

37. The Declaration of Independence refers to "Laws of Nature." James Madison, "No. 51," *The Federalist Papers*, 324; Augustine, *City of God*, 2.4; 5.11; 19.5ff.

38. Thomas Reid, *Practical Ethics*, ed. Knud Haakonssen (Princeton: Princeton University Press, 1990), 177. It is true that at one point in his career Locke did endorse the perpetuity of constitutions (*Fundamental Constitutions of Carolina* [1699–1672], in *The Works of John Locke*, 10 vols. London: Thomas Tegg, 1823], 10:198). However, he was by no means as unambiguous as Reid and Madison in appealing to the concept of tacit consent of citizens in order to authorize the binding character of constitutions on later generations. Thus, in his *Second Treatise on Civil Government* (p. 119), he claimed that because an express consent of a man makes him a member of his society, "a child is born a subject of no country or government."

39. *Notes of Debates*, 353.

40. James Madison, "Letter to Thomas Jefferson" (1790), in *The Papers of Thomas Jefferson* ed. Julian P. Boyd, 28 vols. (Princeton: Princeton University Press, 1961), 16: 149.

41. *Notes of Debates,* 403; James Madison, "No. 54," *The Federalist Papers,* 399; John Locke, *Second Treatise on Civil Government,* 124. Thomas Jefferson ("Letter to P. S. Dupont de Nemours" [1816], in Jefferson, *Writings,* 1386–87) spoke of the right to property. It is true that some scholars, notably Jennifer Nedelsky (*Private Property and the Limits of American Constitutionalism: The Madisonian Framework and Its Legacy* [Chicago: University of Chicago Press, 1990]), have argued that the protection of private property shaped the structure of the American political system. However, Nedelsky (see pp. 262, 271, 330) overlooks the founders' openness toward redistributing property. Also, her contention (pp. 227, 330–31) that economic inequality is the primary source of faction trades on the optimistic anthropological assumptions of the Enlightenment-inspired model. The constitutional system, in fact, presumes that the majority is still a threat to individual rights even if property is shared in common. James Madison, in "No. 10" (*The Federalist Papers,* 79), makes this point explicitly, claiming that "the latent causes of faction are thus sown in the nature of man." He proceeds to list other causes, including religion, government policies, and attachment to different leaders. The check-and-balance system of the Constitution, protecting individuals from the tyranny of factions, is not occasioned merely by property inequalities.

42. Reid, *Practical Ethics,* 208; see also 251, 206. Francis Hutcheson (in a *System of Moral Philosophy* [1755], in *Collected Works of Francis Hutcheson,* 7 vols. [Hildesheim, Germany: G. Olms, 1969–1971], 5:261, 298, 340) affirmed this view, though more like Locke (*Second Treatise on Civil Government,* 124), he rooted all rights in the right of property. Also see Francis Hutcheson, *An Inquiry into the Original of Our Ideas of Beauty and Virtue* (1725) (New York: Garland, 1971), 283ff., as he clearly subordinates the right of property to the common good.

43. Benjamin Franklin, "Letter to Robert Morris" (1783), in Franklin, *Writings,* 1081–82.

44. Thomas Jefferson, "Letter to James Madison" (1785), in Jefferson, *Writings,* 841–42.

45. For an example of these ancient roots, see Martin Luther, *Ordinance of a Common Chest* (1523), in *Luther's Works,* rev. Walther I. Brandt, trans. J. J. Schindel (Philadelphia: Muhlenberg Press, 1962), 45:172. Also see Thomas Reid, "Letter to Dr. James Gregory" (1783), in *The Works of Thomas Reid,* 1: 73.

46. Locke, *Second Treatise on Civil Government,* 31.

47. For a more detailed analysis, which authorizes these conclusions, see Frank Bourgin, *The Great Challenge: The Myth of Laissez-Faire in the Early Republic* (New York: George Braziller, 1989). Also see Page Smith, *The Constitution: A Documentary and Narrative History* (New York: Morrow Quill, 1980), 65–66; McDonald, *Novus Ordo,* 126–27, 135–42; and Richards, *Foundations,* 116–17. For additional primary-source documentation of how the founders envisaged a role for the state in affecting economic policy, see James Madison, "No. 14," *The Federalist Papers,* 102–103; and *Notes of Debates,* 477–78. For a rejection of the claim that socialist propensities in the American system could have been inspired only by the French Revolution, see Smith, *Constitution,* 66. For an analysis of the socialist propensities of that continental revolution, see J. Bronowski and Bruce Mazlish, *The Western Intellectual Tradition: From Leonardo to Hegel* (New York: Harper & Row, 1960), 407–8.

48. For a discussion of these commitment showing how they relate to the Augustinian view of human nature, see Alexander Hamilton, "No. 11," *The Federalist Papers,* 88ff.; Alexander Hamilton, "No. 33," *The Federalist Papers,* 201–205; James Madison, "No. 42," *The Federalist Papers,* esp. 267–68; and James Madison, "No. 44," *The Federalist Papers,* esp. 284.

49. James Madison, "No. 37," *The Federalist Papers,* 226.

Chapter 3

1. *Gallup Poll Monthly,* no. 376 (Jan. 1997), 25–27; *Gallup Poll Monthly,* no. 383 (Aug. 1997), 22–25.

2. *Gallup Poll Monthly,* no. 400 (Jan. 1999), 40; *Gallup Poll Monthly,* no. 418 (July 2000).

3. See chap. 2, n. 33, for references.

4. The Gallup Organization, Government and Public Affairs 1 (30 April 2002).

5. Yankelovich Partners, Inc."General Public Attitudes toward Campaigns and Campaign Practices" (unpublished report from the Center for Congressional and Presidential Studies, April 2000).

6. Richard Sennett, *The Fall of Public Man* (New York: Alfred A. Knopf, 1977), esp. 220, 223, 264–65, 324

7. A. W. Schlegel, *A Course of Lectures on Dramatic Art and Literature,* trans. John Black and A. J. Morrison (London, 1846); Friedrich Schiller, *Uber naïve und sentimentalische Dichtung* (1795).

8. For these insights and the discussion about the celebrity character of leadership that follows, I am indebted to Lawrence M. Friedman, *The Horizontal Society* (New Haven: Yale University Press, 1999), 14–15, 18–19, 28–35, 39–40. Also see Conor Cruise O'Brien, *On the Eve of the Millennium: The Future of Democracy through an Age of Unreason* (New York: Free Press, 1994), 161–62.

9. Yankelovich Partners, Inc., "Are Political Consultants Hurting or Helping Democracy?" (unpublished report from the Center for Congressional and Presidential Studies, American University, June 1999), 20.

10. The survey results of the DDB Needham Life Style Surveys and the Roper Reports are cited in Robert D. Putnam, *Bowling Alone: The Collapse and Revival of American Community* (New York: Simon & Schuster, 2000), 36–37, 448.

11. Putnam, *Bowling Alone,* 38–47.

12. Yankelovich Partners, Inc., "Political Consultants" (unpublished report from the Center for Congressional and Presidential Studies, American University, June 1999), 20–21.

13. Yankelovich Partners, Inc., "General Public Attitudes" (unpublished report from the Center for Congressional and Presidential Studies, American University, April 2000).

14. Ibid.

15. Yankelovich Partners, Inc., "Political Consultants," 23.

16. Carol Whitney, "Campaign Ethics Study Guide" (unpublished instructor's edition, American University, 1999), 6.

17. U.S. Census Bureau, *Statistical Abstract of the United States: 2000,* (Washington, D.C.: USGPO, 2000), 296.

18. For this analysis, I am indebted to Ellen Willis, *Don't Think, Smile!* (Boston: Beacon Press, 1999), 25–28.

19. "Corporate Welfare," *Time*, 9 November 1998, 38.

20. For discussion of how contemporary business theory tends to foster a concern with the present at the expense of the long term, see chap. 5. See also John Maynard Keynes, *The General Theory of Employment, Interest, and Money* (London: Macmillan, 1936), 96–127.

21. Christopher Lasch, *The Culture of Narcissism: American Life in an Age of Diminishing Expectations* (New York: W. W. Norton & Company, 1979), 29–30.

22. Friedman, *Horizontal Society*, 44–45.

23. Ibid., 114–15.

24. James Madison, "No. 10," *The Federalist Papers*, 79.

25. Statistics reported in Barbara Leon Howell, "Wages of Reform," *The Christian Century*, 8–15 May 2002, 27. Also see U.S. Census Bureau, *Statistical Abstract of the United States: 2001*, 433.

26. *Gallup Poll Monthly*, no. 377 (Feb. 1997), 22–23.

27. *Gallup Poll Monthly*, no. 382 (July 1997), 22.

28. U.S. Census Bureau, *Statistical Abstract of the United States: 2001*, 433, 442.

29. "Occupational Employment in Private Industry by Race/Ethnic Group/Sex, United States 1999," <www.eeoc.gov/stats/jobpat/1999/national.html>.

30. Willis, *Don't Think*, 28.

31. Jacques Derrida, *Limited Inc* (Evanston, Ill.: Northwestern University Press, 1988), esp. 144–46, 150–51. See Introduction, n.5.

32. A sophisticated, though ultimately incorrect, version of the critique of such Afrocentric curricula has been offered by Arthur M. Schlesinger Jr. in *The Disuniting of America: Reflections on a Multicultural Society* (New York: W. W. Norton & Company, 1992), 73–99.

33. I was helped to think about these matters by Christopher Lasch, *The Revolt of the Elites and the Betrayal of Democracy* (New York: W. W. Norton & Company, Inc., 1995), 129–40.

34. For this discussion, I am indebted to "The Wild, Wild West," *Time*, 16 July 2001, 18ff.

35. This would be a relatively easy matter to administer in general elections—a bit more delicate in primaries, when numerous candidates, some of them clearly inviable, emerge. If viability were determined by polls too early in primary campaigns, and on that basis some were denied free air time, we would be faced again with the prospect of soaring campaign costs for the first weeks of primary campaigns. Thus the use of polling data to determine viability would need to be done only after a first round of free air time had been granted to all candidates.

36. *Gallup Poll Monthly* <www.gallup.com>, no. 425 (Feb. 2001), 6–7.

Chapter 4

1. For these statistics, I am indebted to Jill Andresky Fraser, *White-Collar Sweatshop: The Deterioration of Work and Its Rewards in Corporate America* (New York: W. W. Norton, 2001), 20.

2. *Gallup Poll Monthly*, no. 403 (April 1999), 31–33.

3. Keynes, *Theory of Employment, Interest, and Money*, 96, 127.

4. Adam Smith, *An Inquiry into the Nature and Causes of the Wealth of Nations*, 8th ed. (London, 1796), 423.

5. See Michael Hardt and Antonio Negri, *Empire* (Cambridge: Harvard University Press, 2000).

6. Scott Leith, "Businesses See Gold in '08 Games," *Atlanta Journal-Constitution*, 14 July 2001.

7. Lawrence M. Friedman, *The Horizontal Society* (New Haven: Yale University Press, 1999), 132–33. For a detailed discussion of how globalization of the economy exploits and effectively colonizes poorer nations, see Joseph Stiglitz, *Globalization and Its Discontents* (New York: W. W. Norton, 2002).

8. U.S. Census Bureau, *Statistical Abstract of the United States: 2000*, 120th ed. (Washington, D.C.: USGPO, 2000), 409.

9. Christopher Lasch, *The Culture of Narcissism: American Life in an Age of Diminishing Expectations* (New York: W. W. Norton & Company, 1979), 139–40.

10. Richard Sennett, *The Corrosion of Character: The Personal Consequences of Work in the New Capitalism* (New York: W. W. Norton & Company, 1998), 48.

11. Ibid., 63.

12. Ibid., 22.

13. For these observations, I am indebted to Sennett, ibid., 48–51.

14. Fraser, *White-Collar Sweatshop*, 116–19.

15. Ibid., 138.

16. Ibid., 163; Sennett, *Corrosion of Character*. The Christian doctrine of realized eschatology (Jer. 31:31; 2 Cor. 5:17; Gal. 6:15), which stresses the radical newness of Christian life, might be a fruitful theme to minister to those victimized by the transitory character of employment in the new economy.

17. Fraser, *White-Collar Sweatshop*, 30–31.

18. These statistics are reported in ibid., 20–21, 119.

19. Ibid., 26.

20. Ellen Willis, *Don't Think, Smile!* (Boston: Beacon Press, 1999), x.

21. Sennett, *Corrosion of Character*, 92.

22. For these insights, I am indebted to Lasch, *Culture of Narcissism*, 124.

23. This point was first brought to my attention by Sennett, *Corrosion of Character*, 110.

24. Ibid., 112–13.

25. Ibid., 116; Richard Rorty, *Contingency, Irony, and Solidarity* (Cambridge: Cambridge University Press, 1989), 73–74.

26. For this discussion, I am indebted to Sennett, *Corrosion of Character*, 111–16.

27. See Fraser, *White-Collar Sweatshop*, 75–76.

28. Ibid., 222.

29. Bureau of Labor Statistics, reported by the Gallup Organization, Religion & Values 1 (5 Feb. 2002).

30. Fraser, *White-Collar Sweatshop*, 40–41.

31. Ibid., 216.

32. *Congressional Quarterly Researcher* (Jan.–Dec. 1999): 1004–5.

33. These statistics, generated by studies by the Center on Budget and Policy Priorities and the Economic Policy Institute, are cited in Fraser, *White-Collar Sweatshop*, 39. They refer to pretax incomes.

34. See ibid., 43, 45–46, for these statistics.

35. Reported in ibid., 68–69.

36. "Health Insurance Coverage 2000 Medical Expenditure Survey," 3 August 2001, at <www.fedstats.gov>. Reported by the Gallup Organization, Health Care 1 (5 March 2002).

37. The statistics for this conclusion are available in the U. S. Census Bureau's *Statistical Abstract of the United States: 2001,* (Washington, D.C.: USGPO, 2001), 1191–92. RAM Research, as reported in "Getting Out of Debt: Introduction" (n.d.) at <www.foo.com>, calculated a month-to-month average of $5,800, credit card debt for the average consumer.

38. For a similar assessment, see Willis, *Don't Think,* 28.

39. Sennett (*Corrosion of Character,* 53–54) provides a helpful discussion of the underlying philosophy of American government interactions with business in comparison to the managed economies of Western Europe.

40. Adam Smith, *The Wealth of Nations* (1776; reprint London: Methuen, 1961), 1:302–03, 07, 09.

41. In making these observations, I have been inspired by Sennett, *Corrosion of Character,* 74–75.

42. Alan Wolfe, *Moral Freedom: The Search for Virtue in a World of Choice* (New York: W. W. Norton, 2001), 97–130.

43. Bill Hendrick, "Boomers and Whoppers," *Atlanta Journal-Constitution,* 15 July 2001.

44. Sennett, *Corrosion of Character,* 23.

45. Lasch, *Culture of Narcissism,* 116–17.

46. Robert Reich, *The Work of Nations,* (New York; Alfred A. Knopf, 1992).

47. United Nations Development Programs, "Quality of Life Index," 2002.

Chapter 5

1. U.S. Census Bureau, *Statistical Abstract of the United States: 2000,* 120th ed. (Washington, D.C.: USGPO, 2000), 289; *Gallup Poll Monthly,* no. 383 (Aug. 1997), 24–25.

2. *Gallup Poll Monthly,* no. 387 (Dec. 1997), 21ff.

3. Barna Research Online, <www.barna.org>,"Religious Beliefs Vary Widely, by Denomination," 25 June 2001, 7; *Gallup Poll Monthly,* no. 383 (Aug. 1997), 51ff.

4. *Gallup Poll Monthly,* no. 411 (Dec. 1999), 50–54.

5. Ibid., no. 431 (Oct. 2001), 51ff.

6. Barna Research Online, "The Year's Most Intriguing Findings, from Barna Research Studies," 17 December 2001, 1.

7. Barna Research Online, "Religious Beliefs," 7; *Gallup Poll Monthly,* no. 426 (March 2001), 9; *Gallup Poll Monthly,* no. 372 (Sept. 1996), 23–24.

8. *Gallup Poll Monthly,* no. 411 (Dec. 1999), 50–54.

9. *Gallup Poll Monthly,* no. 383 (Aug. 1997), 38ff.

10. These statistics are reported in Robert Wuthnow, *The Restructuring of American Religion: Society and Faith since World War II* (Princeton: Princeton University Press, 1988), 88–89.

11. Alan Wolfe, *Moral Freedom: The Search for Virtue in a World of Choice* (New York: W. W. Norton, 2001), 227–28.

12. Ibid., 185.

13. Tom Beaudoin, *Virtual Faith: The Irreverent Spiritual Quest of Generation X* (New York: Jossey-Bass, 1998), 51. For similar attitudes among many Baby Boomers, also

see Wade Clark Roof, *Spiritual Marketplace: Baby Boomers and the Remaking of American Religion* (Princeton: Princeton University Press, 1999).

14. Beaudoin, *Virtual Faith,* chap. 4.

15. George Barna, *What Americans Believe* (Ventura, Calif.: Regal Books, 1991), 185–87.

16. Barna Research Online, "Year's Most Intriguing Findings," 4.

17. Barna Research Online, "Churches Lose Financial Ground in 2000," 5 June 2001.

18. Stephen Carter, *The Culture of Disbelief: How American Law and Politics Trivialize Religious Devotion* (New York: Basic Books, 1993), 44ff.

19. Ibid., 23.

20. Barna Research Online, "Practical Outcomes Replace Biblical Principles as the Moral Standard," 10 September 2001, 1.

21. Barna Research Online, "Researcher Predicts Mounting Challenges to Christian Church," 16 April 2001, 2.

22. For this characterization of the spirituality of the large seeker-oriented churches, I am indebted to the analysis of Donald Miller, *Reinventing American Protestantism: Christianity in the New Millennium* (Berkeley: University of California Press, 1997), 85, 89, 124.

23. A no-less-famed theologian than Karl Barth made this claim in his *Protestant Thought: From Rousseau to Ritschl,* trans. Brian Cozens. (New York: Simon and Schuster, 1959), 306–307. Also see B. A. Gerrish, *A Prince of the Church: Schleiermacher and the Beginnings of Modern Theology* (Philadelphia: Fortress Press, 1984), 1ff.

24. Friedrich Schleiermacher, *Der chirstliche Glaube* (1830), 4, 15–16.

25. Barna Research Online, "Religious Beliefs," 6–7.

26. One of Schleiermacher's modern heirs, Reuel L. Howe, who has had a significant impact on modern pastoral care education, effectively made these points in his *Man's Need and God's Action* (New York: Seabury, 1952), esp. 80ff. Also see Schleiermacher, *Der christliche Glaube,* 271–73.

27. Actually, Catholic openness to the use of historical criticism predates the council; see the papal bull of Pius XII, *Divino Afflante Spiritu.* The Schleiermachian method was unofficially countenanced in Vatican II by the great impact that several theologically liberal Catholics, like Pierre Teilhard de Chardin and Henri de Lubac, had on the council.

28. John Wren-Lewis, "What Are Clergy For?" *The Listener,* 71, no. 1824 (21 March 1964): 418–19.

29. Philip Rieff, *The Triumph of the Therapeutic: Uses of Faith after Freud* (New York: Harper & Row, 1966), 251.

30. This insight was offered by James D. Hunter and Alan Wolfe, as cited in the latter's book, *Moral Freedom,* 182. Sigmund Freud saw the individual's relation to culture in this egocentric way in his *Civilization and Its Discontents,* trans. James Strachey (New York: W. W. Norton, 1961), esp. 86 ff. Also see Erich Fromm, *Man for Himself: An Inquiry into the Psychology of Ethics* (New York: Fawcett World Library, 1947).

31. David Gourlay, "The Churches," *Manchester Guardian,* 23 May 1964, 9.

32. Barna, *What Americans Believe,* 89–90.

33. Some hints of this way of thinking are evident in the work of the great, highly influential German-American proponent of Schleiermacher, Paul Tillich, *Systematic Theology,* 3 volumes in 1 (Chicago: University of Chicago Press, 1967), 2:48. Also see

one of the great early leaders of psychology of religion , David E. Roberts, *Psychotherapy and a Christian View of Man* (New York: Scribner, 1950), 129–38.

34. Christopher Lasch, *The Culture of Narcissism: American Life in an Age of Diminishing Expectations* (New York: W. W. Norton, 1979), 42–43.

35. Lisa Miller, "Redefining God," *Wall Street Journal*, 21 April 2000. See Rosemary Radford Reuther, "Mother Earth and the Megamachine," *Christianity and Crisis* (13 December 1971): 269–72; and James Cone, "Black Theology in American Religion," *Journal of the American Academy of Religion* 53 (Dec. 1985): 768–69.

36. Krister Stendahl, *Paul among Jews and Gentiles, and Other Essays* (Philadelphia: Fortress Press, 1976), 78–96.

37. Barna Research Online, "Religious Beliefs," 6–7.

38. See Carter, *Culture of Disbelief,* 72–73. I wrote the earlier exposé, titled "Inclusiveness in Another Key," *Lutheran Forum* (Lent 1985): 11–15, and received the expressions of concern from sitting bishops in response to that article. It did not mean much three years later.

39. Barna Research Online, "Religious Beliefs," 6–7.

40. Carl S. Dudley and David A. Roozen, "Faith Communities Today" (unpublished report, Hartford Institute for Religion Research, March 2001), 17.

41. Ibid., 57.

Chapter 6

1. *Gallup Poll Monthly*, no. 425 (Feb. 2001), 27. Even after the economic downturn began to register in the polls as the #1 problem, ethics/morality/religion/family still scored high (only after the economy and one percentage point after education) in the next poll (*Gallup Poll Monthly*, no. 430 [July 2001], 55).

2. U.S. Census Bureau, *Statistical Abstract of the United State: 2000,* (Washington, D.C.: USGPO, 2000), 409.

3. I am indebted for these insights to Christopher Lasch, *The Revolt of the Elite: and the Betrayal of Democracy* (New York: W. W. Norton, 1995), 33.

4. *Gallup Poll Monthly*, no. 372 (Sept. 1996), 18–22. Concerning the poll regarding mainline Protestant attitudes, see Barna Research Online, "Practical Outcomes Replace Biblical Principles as the Moral Standard" (10 September 2001), 5.

5. *Gallup Poll Monthly*, no. 386 (Nov. 1997), 4.

6. *Gallup Poll Monthly*, no. 404 (May 1999), 53–55.

7. See Simon LeVay, A Difference in Hypothalmic Structure between Heterosexual and Homosexual Men," *Science* 253 (30 August 1991): 1034–37; and Laura S. Allen and Roger A. Gorski, "Sexual Orientation and the Size of the Anterior Commissure in the Human Brain," *Proceedings of the National Academy of Sciences, USA* 89: 7199–202. Also see Anastasia Toufexis, "The Right Chemistry," *Time*, 15 February 1993, 51; and Shang-Ding Zhang and Ward F. Odenwald, "Misexpression of the white (w) gene triggers male-male courtship in *Drosophila*," *Proceedings of the National Academy of Sciences, USA* 92: 5525–29.

8. *Gallup Poll Monthly*, no. 402 (March 1999), 28–29.

9. "U. S. Adults Postponing Marriage, Census Bureau Reports," U. S. Department of Commerce News, <www.fedstats.gov>, 24 June 2001, 17.

10. For such an assessment, see Lawrence Friedman, *The Horizontal Society* (New Haven: Yale University Press, 1999), 7.

11. For fuller discussions of the history of the evolution of marriage, see Paul Gray, "What Is Love?" *Time*, 15 February 1993, 48; and Robert N. Bellah, William M. Sullivan, Ann Swidler, and Steven M. Tipton, *Habits of the Heart: Individualism and Commitment in American Life* (New York: Harper & Row, 1985), esp. 89.

12. Anthony Walsh, *The Science of Love: Understanding Love and Its Effects on Mind and Body* (Buffalo: Prometheus Books, 1991).

13. This point was first called to my attention intellectually by Christopher Lasch, *The Culture of Narcissism: American Life in an Age of Diminishing Expectations* (New York: W. W. Norton, 1979), 328–29.

14. Ellen Willis, *Don't Think, Smile!* (Boston: Beacon Press, 1999), 106–107.

15. Augustine, *The City of God*, 19.5.

16. U.S. Census Bureau, *Statistical Abstract of the United States: 2000*, 475. A more recent report, noted in *Time*, 30 July 2001, 58, mediated somewhat by population data increases, places the figure at a still-too-high 16 percent.

17. Reported on *60 Minutes*, 19 August 2001.

18. U.S. Census Bureau, *Statistical Abstract of the United States: 2000*, 219. Also see Elizabeth Bartholet, *Nobody's Children* (Boston: Beacon, 1999), 61.

19. U. S. Census Bureau, *Statistical Abstract of the United States: 2001*, 121st ed. (Washington, D.C.: USGPO), 2001, 355; Office of Child Support Enforcement.

20. E. Mavis Hetherington and John Kelly, *For Better or for Worse: Divorce Reconsidered* (New York: W. W. Norton, 2002).

21. Penelope Leach, cited in David Frum, *How We Got Here: The '70s* (New York: Basic Books, 2000), 111; also consider the suppositions of Parent Effectiveness Training techniques.

22. Lasch, *Culture of Narcissism*, 283.

23. Ibid., 291.

24. Frum, *How We Got Here*, 109.

25. Lasch, *Culture of Narcissism*, 102.

26. Frum, *How We Got Here*, 109.

27. Federal Interagency on Child and Family Statistics, <www.childstats.gov>, "America's Children: Key National Indicators of Well-Being, 2000."

28. Ibid.

29. Department of Health and Human Services, <www.hhs.gov>, "HHS News," 19 Dec. 2001; National Institute on Drug Abuse, <www.drugabuse.gov>, "NIDA Notes," Nov. 1999, 2.

30. Frum, *How We Got Here*, 111. For details of the University of Michigan study, see Sonja Lewis, "Protective parent, busy schedules leave children little time to savor season," *Atlanta Journal-Constitution*, 28 June 2002.

31. Frum, *How We Got Here*, 111.

32. Laura Vanderkam, "Hookups Starve the Soul," *USA Today*, 26 July 2001, based on a study by the Institute on American Values.

33. Reinhold Niebuhr, *Justice and Mercy*, ed. Ursula M. Niebuhr (repr., Louisville: Westminster/John Knox, 1991), 40–41.

34. Martin Luther, *Sermons*, in *D. Martin Luthers Werke, kritische Gesamtausgabe* (Weimar: Hermann Böhlaus, 1883), 24:591ff.

35. Martin Luther, *The Sermon on the Mount* (1521), in *Works*, ed. Jaroslav Pelikan, 55 vols. (St. Louis: Concordia, 1955), 21:98.

36. Benjamin Franklin, *Poor Richard Improved* (1750), in Benjamin Franklin, *Writings* (New York: The Library of America, 1987), 1259.

37. Robert D. Putnam, *Bowling Alone: The Collapse and Revival of American Community* (New York: Simon & Schuster, 2000), 332–4.

Chapter 7

1. These dynamics were first called to my attention by Christopher Lasch, *The Culture of Narcissism: American Life in an Age of Diminishing Expectations* (New York: W. W. Norton, 1979), 311–12.

2. Allan Bloom, *The Closing of the American Mind: How Higher Education Has Failed Democracy and Impoverished the Souls of Today's Students* (New York: Simon and Schuster, 1987), 156.

3. *Statistical Abstract of the United States: 2000*, (Washington, D.C.: USGPO, 2000), 289.

4. *Gallup Poll Monthly*, no. 430 (July 2001), 55; cf. *Gallup Poll Monthly*, no. 425 (Feb. 2001), 6–7.

5. John Leo, *Incorrect Thoughts: Notes on Our Wayward Culture* (New Brunswick, N.J.: Transaction Publishers, 2001), 47–48. The poor academic quality of such education courses is suggested by the fact that most of them ranked among college courses with the highest rates of A's in a U.S. Department of Education study: Clifford Adelman, *The New College Course Map and Transcript Files: Changes in Course-Taking and Achievement, 1972–1993*, 2d ed. (Washington, D.C.: U.S. Dept. of Education, Office of Educational Research and Improvement, 1999), 209.

6. *Gallup Poll Monthly*, no. 394 (July 1998), 31.

7. Reported in David Frum, *How We Got Here: The 70s* (New York: Basic Books, 2000), 141.

8. Adelman, *New College Course Map*, 198–99.

9. U. S. Department of Education, Office of Educational Research and Improvement, National Center for Educational Statistics, *The Nation's Report Card: Mathematics 2000* (Washington, D.C.: NCES, 2001).

10. For these insights, I am indebted to Christopher Lasch, *The Revolt of the Elite: and the Betrayal of Democracy* (New York: W. W. Norton, 1995), 158–59.

11. U.S. Census Bureau, *Statistical Abstract of the United States: 2000*, 194. There were 176,307 education graduates in 1971, and only 105,223 in 1997. By contrast, business graduates doubled in this period, to 226,633.

12. U.S. Supreme Court, *Lemon* v. *Kurtzman* (1971), in *U.S. Documents*, vol. 403, 602.

13. George Will, reporting on a speech by Lynne Cheney, in the *Atlanta-Journal Constitution*, 23 Dec. 2001.

14. Bloom, *Closing*, 61.

15. Lasch, *Revolt of the Elites*, esp. 176–77.

16. Bloom, *Closing*, esp. 141ff.

17. Immanuel Kant, *Critique of Pure Reason*, trans. Norman Kemp Smith (New York: St. Martin's, 1965), 41–62, 87–89, 257–75.

18. For such an assessment of the connections between Schleiermacher and Kant, see Karl Barth, *Protestant Thought: From Rousseau to Ritschl*, trans. Brian Cozens (New York: Simon and Schuster, 1959), esp. 344.

19. For these insights, I am indebted to Bloom, *Closing*, 146–47. For the roots of these concepts in these Enlightenment figures, see Max Weber, *The Protestant Ethic and the Spirit of Capitalism* (1904–05); Friedrich Nietzsche, *Thus Spoke Zarathustra*

(1892), I. Pro. 4, in Walter Kaufmann, ed., *The Portable Nietzsche* (New York: Viking, 1954), 128; Nietzsche, in *The Portable Nietzsche.*, I. Speech. 4,16, 147, 173; Friedrich Nietzsche, *Towards a Genealogy of Morals* (1887), in *The Portable Nietzsche*, 451.

20. See pp. 63–64.

21. For helping me to recognize these dynamics, I am indebted to Lasch, *Revolt of the Elites*, 12–14, 184. For the premier spokesperson for deconstruction and indications of how he has been interpreted in America, see Jacques Derrida, *Limited Inc* (Evanston, Ill.: Northwestern University Press, 1977), 105–106, 131, 145. Also see Edward Said, (*Orientalism* [New York: Vintage, 1994], esp. 10), who claims standards are never disinterested acts of judgment but always assertions of power grounded in ideology and self-interest.

22. See Leo, *Incorrect Thoughts*, 72–74, 91–95.

23. These developments were noted by Lasch, *Revolt of the Elites*, 192–93.

24. For Madison's reflections on the human propensity to such sloth, see pp. 58–59.

Conclusion

1. See Introduction, n. 25, for references.

2. Reported in Robert D. Putnam, *Bowling Alone: The Collapse and Revival of American Community* (New York: Simon & Schuster, 2000), 332–34. Also see chap. 6, n. 9.

3. See chap. 2, n. 35, for the founders' appeal to natural law. Such an appeal is also implied in the Declaration of Independence. For Augustine, see *The City of God* (413–26), 14.28; 18.2; 19.5ff.

4. Augustine, *The Confessions* (397), 13.28.43.

5. See pp. 53ff.

6. Conor Cruise O'Brien, *On the Eve of the Millennium: The Future of Democracy through an Age of Unreason* (New York: Free Press, 1994), 156.

7. Thomas Reid, *Essays on the Intellectual Powers of Man* (1785), in *The Works of Thomas Reid D.D.*, 7th ed., 2 vols. in 1 (Edinburgh: Maclachlan and Stewart, 1872), 1:364, 403, 437–38; and Reid, *Essays on the Active Powers of Man* (1788), in *Works*, 2:640, 589, 591, 595.

8. George Barna, *What Americans Believe* (Ventura, Calif.: Regal Books, 1991), 83–85; "The Year's Most Intriguing Findings, from Barna Research Studies," 17 December 2001, 2.

9. Robert Wuthnow, *Acts of Compassion: Caring for Others and Helping Ourselves* (Princeton: Princeton University Press, 1991); Wuthnow, *Sharing the Journey: Support Groups and America's New Quest for Community* (New York: Free Press, 1994), 45–46, 59–76, 170, 320; and Putnam, *Bowling Alone*, 129, 132–33.

Index

African Americans 30,
85–92, 93, 110, 112,
132, 137, 138, 148–49,
176, 177, 183
African Methodist Episcopal
Zion Church 137
Ahlstrom, Sydney E. 44,
192n. 25, 193nn. 2, 4
Assemblies of God 137
Augustine 11, 16, 32, 33, 34,
36–41, 42, 43, 44, 46–49,
51–52, 54–55, 56, 57–63,
65–67, 70, 71, 77, 78, 80,
83, 84, 85–86, 91–92, 93,
96–97, 102, 115–17, 119,
120, 122, 127–28, 133,
134, 137–39, 141–44,
147–49, 154–57, 159,
170, 174, 175, 178, 179,
181, 183–88, 189n. 5,
191nn. 6, 7, 9–13,
192nn. 18–20, 22, 24,
26, 193n. 1, 194n. 8,
195nn. 25, 37, 197n. 15,
205nn. 3, 4

baby boom generation 16,
18, 29, 31–32, 99,
124–25, 133, 149, 187,
200–1n. 13
Barna Research Group
120–21, 123, 124–25,
127, 134, 137–38,
187nn. 3, 6, 7, 201nn.
15–17, 20, 21, 25, 32,
202nn. 37, 39, 205n. 8
Barth, Karl 41, 191n. 26,
192n. 19, 201n. 23,
204n. 18
biblical authority

theological method 120,
121, 124–34, 137–39,
173–74, 187–88
Bill of Rights 56, 63, 65
Bloom, Allan 17, 162–63,
172, 173, 190nn. 5, 8,
204nn. 2, 14, 16, 19
Bush, George 14, 71, 74, 80,
105
Bush, George W. 14, 71, 82,
88, 93, 102, 111, 152
business 69–71, 81–82,
83–84, 88, 90–91, 93,
94–95, 119, 134–37,
147, 151, 152, 159–60,
167–70, 176–77, 181,
183, 200n. 39

campaign finance reform
81–82, 92–96, 110–11
capitalism, free market
23–24, 83, 84, 92, 101,
102, 111, 183
Carter, Stephen 123–24,
201nn. 18–19, 202n. 38
children 22, 30, 31, 87, 101,
141, 142, 146, 148,
149–56, 159, 160–63,
168, 172, 177–78, 179
Christian Church Disciples of
Christ 123
Christian Methodist Episcopal Church 123
Christianity, in America 14,
15, 33–34, 42, 44–45,
91, 100, 119–39, 145,
174, 185, 186, 192n. 25
Church of God—Cleveland,
Tenn. 137
Church of God in Christ
137, 192n. 26

clergy 13–31, 119–20,
130–31, 135, 145
Clinton, William 21, 26, 74,
75, 76, 88, 93, 99, 102,
116, 190n. 18
common sense
See Scottish Common
Sense Realism
computers 16, 26, 96, 102,
105, 108, 112, 167, 172,
177
Constitution, U.S. 1, 2, 14,
16, 32, 43, 46, 51, 53,
54, 55, 56, 57–58, 60–61,
63, 65–66, 67, 80, 84, 94,
96, 97, 116, 127–28,
138, 139, 167, 170, 175,
177, 179, 18, 184, 185,
187, 189n. 5, 196n. 41
Constitutional Convention
58, 61, 195 nn. 26, 29,
39, 196nn. 41, 47
consumer spending 23, 109,
110, 115, 189n. 2
cynicism 13, 16, 46, 47, 49,
60–70, 77, 80, 115–16,
184, 185, 188

Declaration of Independence
56, 60, 139, 195n. 37,
205n. 3
deconstruction 89, 176,
205n. 21
divorce 29, 130–32, 141, 143,
147, 148, 157
drugs 24, 81, 152

ecology 62–63, 93
economics 14, 15, 23–24, 55,
62–65, 75, 83–84, 88,

90–91, 99–117, 142, 148, 163, 183, 189nn. 2, 3, 190n. 12, 194n. 11, 198n. 20, 199n. 16, 202n. 1

educational system, in America 15, 81, 85, 91, 100, 102, 115, 130, 131, 139, 153, 159–71, 177–79, 202n. 1

higher education 16, 17, 85, 110, 119, 154, 159, 163, 165, 167, 171–77, 179

educational bureaucracy 102, 167–70

Ellingsen, Mark 41, 192nn. 16, 25, 194n. 11, 202n. 38

enlightenment 32, 48, 51, 54, 56, 58–59, 65, 66, 83, 102, 116, 120, 125, 126, 127, 149, 156, 176, 178, 185, 186, 191n. 26, 196n. 41

in Germany 16, 32, 119, 139, 141, 173–75, 177, 181, 186, 187

Episcopal Church 44, 123

Evangelical Free Church in America 137

Evangelical Lutheran Church in America 136

The Federalist Papers 57, 58, 60, 65–66, 195nn. 24, 28, 30–36, 196nn. 41, 47, 197nn. 48, 49, 198n. 24

Franklin, Benjamin 53, 55, 56, 64, 157, 193n. 8, 194n. 19, 195n. 27, 196n. 43, 203n. 36

Fraser, Jill Andresky 198n. 1, 199nn. 14–19, 27, 28, 30, 31, 33–35

free will, and its bondage 34, 36–37, 38, 45, 48, 49, 191n. 8

Freud, Sigmund 16–17, 73, 174, 181, 201n. 30

Friedman, Lawrence M. 190n. 19, 197n. 8,

198nn. 22, 23, 199n. 7, 202n. 10

Frum, David 153, 203nn. 21, 24, 26, 30, 31, 204n. 7

Gallup Poll 14, 23, 25, 29, 70, 71, 87, 96, 100, 119–22, 142, 143, 146, 163, 189n. 3, 190n. 14, 197nn. 2, 4, 198nn. 26, 27, 36, 2, 199n. 29, 200nn. 36, 1–5, 7–10, 202nn. 1, 4–6, 8, 204nn. 4, 6

gay rights 130–31, 145–46, 156

Generation X 78, 122–25, 133, 187

Hamilton, Alexander 58–60, 194n. 16, 195nn. 34, 35, 197n. 48

Hispanic–Americans Latinos 30, 90, 138, 183

homosexuality *See* gay rights

human rights/civil liberties 56, 63, 102–103, 145, 175–76

humanities 160, 171–172, 175–77

individualism 17, 24, 28, 122, 182

International Church of the Foursquare Gospel 137

Islam 103, 124

Jefferson, Thomas 52, 53, 55, 57, 193nn. 3, 5, 6, 9, 10, 194nn. 11, 20, 195nn. 21, 23, 24, 196nn. 40, 44

Judaism 120, 124, 174, 184–85

justice 38–39, 60–61, 82, 90, 117, 183, 184

justification, by grace through faith 36, 36, 48, 134, 137–38

Kant, Immanuel 89, 173, 175, 181, 186, 189–90n. 5, 191n. 26, 204nn. 17, 18

Keynes, John Maynard 64–65, 101–2, 198nn. 20, 3

King, Martin Luther, Jr. 13, 38–39, 88–89, 189n. 1

labor unions 95, 107–9, 117

Lasch, Christopher 15–16, 82–83, 114–15, 189n. 4, 190nn. 9, 11, 18, 191n. 22, 198nn. 21, 33, 199n. 22, 200n. 45, 202nn. 34, 3, 203nn. 13, 22, 23, 25, 204nn. 1, 10, 15, 205nn. 21, 23

law of God 39, 61, 133

natural law 54, 60, 61, 139, 184, 194n. 18, 195n. 37, 205n. 3

Locke, John 52, 53–55, 56, 61, 63, 65, 184, 186, 191n. 26, 194nn. 12–16, 195n. 38, 196nn. 41, 46

Luther, Martin 39, 46, 155, 157, 191n. 13, 192n. 23, 196n. 45, 203nn. 34–35

Madison, James 13, 16, 46, 51, 52, 55, 58–62, 64–67, 71, 83, 155, 156, 179, 189n. 5, 193n. 2, 194n. 18, 195nn. 22, 24–26, 28–33, 36–39, 196nn. 40, 46, 47, 197nn. 48, 49, 198n. 24, 205n. 24

marriage 29, 42, 130–131, 141–43, 146–50, 156–57, 163, 182, 202n. 1, 203n. 11

media 13, 22, 24–26, 63, 69, 70, 72, 74, 76, 77–79, 81, 95–96, 115, 119, 122–23, 130, 153, 163, 167, 172–73, 177

meritocracy 22, 26–27, 32, 116, 135–36, 190n. 18

middle class 14, 28, 30, 67, 84, 85, 88, 91, 97, 109, 110, 150, 154, 172, 189n. 2

Montesquieu, Baron de Secondat, Charles–Louis de 54–55, 194n. 18

narcissism 15–16, 18–32, 33, 70, 72–74, 76, 79, 82, 83, 85, 88, 101, 109, 111–15, 120, 122, 132, 139, 141, 143–44, 146–47, 148, 149, 151, 159–60, 162–67, 174, 182–83
Niebuhr, H. Richard 192n. 25, 195n. 25
Niebuhr, Reinhold 13, 46–48, 189n. 1, 193nn. 31, 33, 203n. 33
Nietzsche, Friedrich 174, 181, 204–5n. 19
nihilism 69, 89, 174

optimism (optimistic view of human nature) 16, 31, 47–48, 51–54, 56–59, 65–67, 70, 78, 80, 116, 119, 120, 122, 126–28, 131–32, 134, 141, 149, 154, 174–78, 181, 183–86, 193n. 1

parenting
    permissiveness 101, 142, 146, 148–56, 164, 166, 168–70, 178
Pelagius 34, 36, 48, 191n. 5
political correctness 17, 130, 151, 156, 163, 175, 177
politics, in America 15, 69–97, 101, 110–11, 198n. 35, 200n. 39
poverty 14, 27, 30–31, 64, 65, 67, 81, 83–88, 91, 97, 109, 110, 116, 148, 149, 183
    See also welfare
Presbyterian Church U.S.A. 44
Puritanism 44, 45, 52, 58, 73, 192n. 25
Putnam, Robert 157, 187, 197nn. 10, 11, 294n. 37, 205nn. 2, 9

Quakers See Society of Friends

Racism 30, 82, 86–92, 110
Reagan, Ronald 14, 31, 75, 85

Reid, Thomas 45, 52, 62–64, 192n. 27, 192–93n. 28, 195n. 38, 196nn. 42, 45, 205n. 7
relativism 16–17, 89, 173–76, 182, 183, 186–87
religion in America 23, 119–39, 145, 183
    in schools 170
Religious Right 81, 124, 131
Richards, David A. J. 194n. 18, 196n. 47
Roman Catholic Church 119, 127–28, 134–35, 137–38, 201n. 27
romanticism 73, 126, 128–29
Roosevelt, Franklin D. 74–75, 101–2

SAT 159–61, 171–72
Schleiermacher, Friedrich 126–29, 132–34, 137, 201nn. 24, 26, 27, 33, 204n. 18
Scottish Common Sense Realism 45–46, 52, 61, 63, 64, 186, 193n. 2
Sennett, Richard 72–74, 107, 189n. 2, 197n. 6, 199nn. 10–13, 16, 21, 23, 26, 200nn. 39, 41, 44
separation of powers 55, 59–61, 65, 196n. 41
sex 21, 25–26, 29, 40–41, 76, 81, 130–31, 141–46, 148, 154, 156
sin
    concupiscence 32–49, 56, 58, 63, 67, 71, 72, 116, 122, 127, 131–32, 137, 155, 156, 170, 176, 178, 183–85, 188, 192nn. 19, 23, 205n. 24
    original sin 13, 32, 33–37, 41–42, 45, 48, 58, 132, 133, 138, 178, 184, 187, 189n. 5, 195n. 30
Smith, Adam 64–65, 111, 198n. 4, 200n. 40
Society of Friends 45
Southern Baptist Convention 45, 120
standardized testing 161, 166, 168–70

Statistical Abstract of the United States 187, 190n. 10, 191n. 23, 197n. 17, 198nn. 25, 28, 199n. 8, 200nn. 37, 1, 202n. 2, 203nn. 16, 18, 19, 204nn. 3, 11

tax structure 82, 85–86, 111, 156, 159, 169
team management models 15, 79, 104, 106–9, 111–15, 135–36, 177
terrorism 71, 82, 103, 120–21
therapeutic ethos, in America 16–19, 22, 26, 30, 32–34, 72–74, 79, 80, 113–14, 119–26, 128–30, 132–35, 141, 148–51, 153, 156, 161, 164–67, 170–76, 183

United Church of Christ 44, 46, 123, 136
United Methodist Church 44, 123, 136, 192n. 26

Weber, Max 174, 181, 204n. 19
welfare 64, 81, 83, 85–86, 131, 152, 196n. 41
    See also poverty
whole–language approach 161–64
Willis, Ellen 197n. 18, 199n. 20, 203n. 14
Wills, Gary 192n. 28, 193nn. 3, 4, 7, 194n. 11, 198n. 30, 200n. 38
Witherspoon, John 45–46, 52, 193nn. 29, 30, 195n. 25
Wolfe, Alan 113, 200nn. 42, 11, 12, 201n. 30
women's rights/equality 14, 104, 130–31, 142, 151, 156, 177

Yankelovich Partners Inc. 71–72, 78, 197nn. 5, 9, 12